PLOTINUS
ENNEAD I.6

THE *ENNEADS* OF PLOTINUS
With Philosophical Commentaries

Series Editors: John M. Dillon, Trinity College, Dublin
and Andrew Smith, University College, Dublin

ALSO AVAILABLE IN THE SERIES:

FORTHCOMING TITLES IN THE SERIES INCLUDE:

PLOTINUS
ENNEAD I.6

On Beauty

Translation with an Introduction
and Commentary

ANDREW SMITH

PARMENIDES
PUBLISHING

Las Vegas | Zurich | Athens

PARMENIDES PUBLISHING
Las Vegas | Zurich | Athens

This edition published in 2016 by Parmenides Publishing
in the United States of America

ISBN soft cover: 978–1–930972–93-3
ISBN e-Book: 978–1–930972–94-0

Library of Congress Cataloging-in-Publication Data

Names: Plotinus, author. | Smith, Andrew, 1945- translator, commentator.
Title: Ennead I.6 : on beauty / Plotinus ; translation with an introduction
  and commentary, Andrew Smith.
Other titles: Ennead. I, 6. English | On beauty
Description: First edition. | Las Vegas, Nevada : Parmenides Publishing,
  2016. | Series: The Enneads of Plotinus with philosophical commentaries |
  Includes bibliographical references and index.
Identifiers: LCCN 2015045319 (print) | LCCN 2015051009 (ebook) | ISBN
  9781930972933 (pbk. : alk. paper) | ISBN 9781930972940 (ebook)
Subjects: LCSH: Plotinus. Ennead. I, 6. | Aesthetics, Ancient--Early works to
  1800.
Classification: LCC B693.E52 E5 2016 (print) | LCC B693.E52 (ebook) | DDC
  186/.4--dc23
LC record available at http://lccn.loc.gov/2015045319

Cover image © Arnold Hermann and Light & Night Studios
www.lightandnight.com – Statue of a Muse ("Munich Clio"),
Glyptothek Munich, Germany

Typeset in Warnock and Futura by Parmenides Publishing
Printed and lay-flat bound by Edwards Brothers Malloy, Ann Arbor, MI

www.parmenides.com

Contents

For Margaret and Anna

Introduction to the Series
With a Brief Outline of the Life and Thought of Plotinus (205–270 CE)

Plotinus was born in 205 CE in Egypt of Greek-speaking parents. He attended the philosophical schools in Alexandria where he would have studied Plato (427–347 BCE), Aristotle (384–322 BCE), the Stoics and Epicureans as well as other Greek philosophical traditions. He began his serious philosophical education, however, relatively late in life, at the age of twenty-seven and was deeply impressed by the Platonist Ammonius Saccas about whom we, unfortunately, know very little, but with whom Plotinus studied for some eleven years. Even our knowledge of Plotinus' life is limited to what we can glean from Porphyry's introduction to his edition of his philosophical treatises, an account colored by Porphyry's own concerns. After completing his studies in Alexandria Plotinus attempted, by joining a military expedition of the Roman emperor Gordian III, to make contact with the

Brahmins in order to learn something of Indian thought. Unfortunately Gordian was defeated and killed (244). Plotinus somehow managed to extract himself and we next hear of him in Rome where he was able to set up a school of philosophy in the house of a high-ranking Roman lady by the name of Gemina. It is, perhaps, surprising that he had no formal contacts with the Platonic Academy in Athens, which was headed at the time by Longinus, but Longinus was familiar with his work, partly at least through Porphyry who had studied in Athens. The fact that it was Rome where Plotinus set up his school may be due to the originality of his philosophical activity and to his patrons. He clearly had some influential contacts, not least with the philhellenic emperor Gallienus (253–268), who may also have encouraged his later failed attempt to set up a civic community based on Platonic principles in a ruined city in Campania.

Plotinus' school was, like most ancient schools of philosophy, relatively small in scale, but did attract distinguished students from abroad and from the Roman upper classes. It included not only philosophers but also politicians and members of the medical profession who wished to lead the philosophical life. His most famous student was Porphyry (233–305) who, as a relative late-comer to the school, persuaded him to put into writing the results of his seminars. It is almost certain that we possess most, if not all of his written output, which represents his mature thought, since he didn't commence writing until the age of forty-eight. The school seemingly had inner and outer circles, and Plotinus himself was clearly an inspiring and sympathetic teacher who took a deep interest in the philosophical and spiritual progress of his students. Porphyry tells us that when he was suffering from severe depression Plotinus straight away visited him in his lodgings to help him. His concern for others is also illustrated by the fact that he was entrusted with the personal education of many orphans and the care of their property and careers. The reconciliation of this worldly involvement with the encouragement to lead a life of contemplation is encapsulated in Porphyry's comment that "he was present to himself and others at the same time."

The *Enneads* of Plotinus is the edition of his treatises arranged by his pupil Porphyry who tried to put shape to the collection he had inherited by organizing it into six sets of nine treatises (hence the name *"Enneads")* that led the reader through the levels of Plotinus' universe, from the physical world to Soul, Intellect and, finally, to the highest principle, the One. Although Plotinus undoubtedly had a clearly structured metaphysical system by the time he began committing himself to expressing his thought in written form, the treatises themselves are not systematic expositions, but rather explorations of particular themes and issues raised in interpreting Plato and other philosophical texts read in the School. In fact, to achieve his neat arrangement Porphyry was sometimes driven even to dividing certain treatises (e.g., III.2–3; IV.3–5, and VI.4–5).

Although Plotinus' writings are not transcripts of his seminars, but are directed to the reader, they do, nevertheless, convey the sort of lively debate that he encouraged in his school. Frequently he takes for granted that a particular set of ideas is already familiar as having been treated in an earlier seminar that may or may not be found in the written text. For this reason it is useful for the reader to have some idea of the main philosophical principles of his system as they can be extracted from the *Enneads* as a whole.

Plotinus regarded himself as a faithful interpreter of Plato whose thought lies at the core of his entire project. But Plato's thought, whilst definitive, does according to Plotinus require careful exposition and clarification, often in the light of other thinkers such as Aristotle and the Stoics. It is because of this creative application of different traditions of ancient thought to the interpretation of Plato that Plotinus' version of Platonism became, partly through the medium of later Platonists such as Porphyry, Iamblichus (245–325), and Proclus (412–485), an influential source and way of reading both Plato and Aristotle in the Middle Ages, the Renaissance, and up to the early 19th century, when scholars first began to differentiate Plato and "Neoplatonism." His thought, too, provided early Christian theologians of the Latin and particularly of the Byzantine tradition, with a rich variety of metaphysical concepts with which to explore and express difficult doctrinal ideas. His fashioning of Plato's ideas into a consistent metaphysical structure, though no longer accepted as a uniquely valid way of approaching Plato, was influential in promoting the notion of metaphysical systems in early modern philosophy. More recently increasing interest has centered on his exploration of the self, levels of consciousness, and his expansion of discourse beyond the levels of normal ontology to the examination of what lies both above and beneath being. His thought continues to challenge us when confronted with the issue of man's nature and role in the universe and of the extent and limitations of human knowledge.

Whilst much of Plotinus' metaphysical structure is recognizably an interpretation of Plato it is an interpretation that is not always immediately obvious just because it is filtered through several centuries of developing Platonic thought, itself already overlaid with important concepts drawn from other schools. It is, nevertheless, useful as a starting point to see how Plotinus attempts to bring coherence to what he believed to be a comprehensive worldview expressed in the Platonic dialogues. The Platonic Forms are central. They become for him an intelligible universe that is the source and model of the physical universe. But aware of Aristotle's criticism of the Platonic Forms as lifeless causes he takes on board Aristotle's concept of god as a self-thinker to enable him to identify this intelligible universe as a divine Intellect that thinks itself as the Forms or Intelligibles. The doctrine of the Forms as the thoughts of god had already entered Platonism, but not as the rigorously argued identity that Plotinus proposed. Moreover the Intelligibles, since they are identical with Intellect, are themselves actively intellectual; they are intellects. Thus Plato's world of Forms has become a complex and dynamic intelligible universe in which unity and plurality, stability, and activity are reconciled.

Now although the divine Intellect is one it also embraces plurality, both because its thoughts, the Intelligibles, are many and because it may itself be analyzed into thinker and thought. Its unity demands a further principle, which is the cause of its unity. This principle, which is the cause of all unity and being but does not possess unity or being in itself, he calls the One, an interpretation of the Idea of the Good in Plato's *Republic* that is "beyond being" and that may be seen as the simple (hence "one") source of all reality. We thus have the first two of what subsequently became known as the three Hypostases, the One, Intellect, and Soul, the last of which acts as an intermediary between the intelligible and physical universes. This last Hypostasis takes on all the functions of transmitting form and life that may be found in Plato, although Plato himself does not always make such a clear distinction between soul and intellect. Thus the One is the ultimate source of all, including this universe, which is then prefigured in Intellect and transmitted through Soul to become manifest as our physical universe. Matter, which receives imperfectly this expression, is conceived not as an independently existing counter-principle, a dangerously dualist notion, but is in a sense itself a product of the One, a kind of non-being that, while being nothing specific in itself, nevertheless is not simply not there.

But this procession from an ultimate principle is balanced by a return movement at each level of reality that fully constitutes itself only when it turns back in contemplation of its producer. And so the whole of reality is a dynamic movement of procession and return, except for matter, which has no life of its own to make this return; it is inert. This movement of return, which may be traced back to the force of "love" in Plato or Aristotle's final cause, is characterized by Plotinus as a cognitive activity, a form of contemplation, weaker at each successive level, from Intellect through discursive reasoning to the merest image of rational order as expressed in the objects of the physical universe.

The human individual mirrors this structure to which we are all related at each level. For each of us has a body and soul, an intellect, and even something within us that relates to the One. While it is the nature of soul to give life to body, the higher aspect of our soul also has aspirations toward intellect, the true self, and even beyond. This urge to return corresponds to the cosmic movement of return. But the tension between soul's natural duty to body and its origins in the intelligible can be, for the individual, a source of fracture and alienation in which the soul becomes over-involved and overwhelmed by the body and so estranged from its true self. Plotinus encourages us to make the return or ascent, but at the same time attempts to resolve the conflict of duties by reconciling the two-fold nature of soul as life-giving and contemplative.

This is the general framework within which important traditional philosophical issues are encountered, discussed and resolved, but always in a spirit of inquiry and ongoing debate. Issues are frequently encountered in several different contexts, each angle providing a different insight. The nature of the soul and its relationship to the body is examined at length (IV) using the Aristotelian distinctions of levels of soul (vegetative, growth, sensitive, rational) whilst maintaining the immortal nature of the transcendent soul in Platonic terms. The active nature of the soul in sense-perception is maintained to preserve the principle that incorporeals cannot be affected by corporeal reality. A vigorous discussion (VI.4 and 5) on the general nature of the relationship of incorporeals to body explores in every detail and in great depth the way in which incorporeals act on body. A universe that is the product of design is reconciled with the freedom of the individual. And, not least, the time-bound nature of the physical universe and human reason is grounded in the life of Intellect, which subsists in eternity. Sometimes, however, Plotinus seems to break outside the framework of traditional metaphysics: the nature of matter and the One, each as non-being, though in a different sense, strains the terminology and structure of traditional ontology; and the attempt to reconcile the role of the individual soul within the traditional Platonic distinction of transcendent and immanent reality leads to a novel exploration of the nature of the self, the "I."

It is this restless urge for exploration and inquiry that lends to the treatises of Plotinus their philosophical vitality. Whilst presenting us with a rich and complexly coherent system, he constantly engages us in philosophical inquiry. In this way each treatise presents us with new ideas and fresh challenges. And, for Plotinus, every philosophical engagement is not just a mental exercise but also contributes to the rediscovery of the self and our reintegration with the source of all being, the Platonic aim of "becoming like god."

While Plotinus, like Plato, always wishes to engage his audience to reflect for themselves, his treatises are not easy reading, partly no doubt because his own audience was already familiar with many of his basic ideas and, more importantly, had been exposed in his seminars to critical readings of philosophical texts that have not survived to our day. Another problem is that the treatises do not lay out his thought in a systematic way but take up specific issues, although always the whole system may be discerned in the background. Sometimes, too, the exact flow of thought is difficult to follow because of an often condensed mode of expression.

Because we are convinced that Plotinus has something to say to us today, we have launched this series of translations and commentaries as a means of opening up the text to readers with an interest in grappling with the philosophical issues revealed by an encounter with Plotinus' own words and arguments. Each volume will contain a new translation, careful summaries of the arguments and structure of the treatise, and a philosophical commentary that will aim to throw light on the philosophical meaning and import of the text.

John M. Dillon
Andrew Smith

Abbreviations

Armstrong   Armstrong, A. H. 1966–1982. *Plotinus.* Greek Text with English Translation and Introductions. Cambridge (MA): Loeb.

Bréhier   Bréhier, É. 1924–1938. *Plotin, Ennéades.* Greek Text and French Translation with Introductions and Notes. Paris: Les Belles.

HS$_1$ Henry, P. and Schwyzer, H.-R. 1951–1973. *Plotini Opera* I-III (editio maior). Paris: Desclée de Brouwer et Cie.

HS$_2$ Henry, P. and Schwyzer, H.-R. 1964–1982. *Plotini Opera* I-III (editio minor, with revised text). Oxford: Clarendon Press.

HS$_3$ Henry, P. and Schwyzer, H.-R. 1973. *Addenda et Corrigenda ad textum et apparatum lectionum.* In HS$_1$, t. III.

HS₄   Henry, P. and Schwyzer, H.-R. 1982. *Addenda et Corrigenda ad textum et apparatum lectionum.* In HS₂, t. III.

HS₅   Schwyzer, H.-R. 1987. "Corrigenda ad Plotini Textum." *Museum Helveticum* 44, 181–210.

SVF   Von Arnim, H., ed. 1905–1924. *Stoicorum Veterum Fragmenta.* Leipzig: Teubner.

Acknowledgments

THE AUTHOR WOULD LIKE TO THANK his co-editor, John Dillon, for helpful remarks on a draft of this work, and Eliza Tutellier, Sara Hermann, and Gale Carr for their editorial support in the production of this volume and of the series as a whole.

Introduction to the Treatise

ALTHOUGH THIS TREATISE WAS THE FIRST to be composed by Plotinus, we must bear in mind that it was written in his fifties, when he had already established the main outlines of his thought, which are implied throughout the treatise and surface at different stages of the exposition. It should, therefore, be read in the context of his grand metaphysical framework. And although the title, supplied by Porphyry, may suggest a work on aesthetics and thus of limited focus, this is far from the case. For it quickly becomes apparent that Plotinus' main interest is in transcendent beauty, which he identifies with the Good, the goal of all philosophical endeavor in the Platonist's search to assimilate himself with the divine. The treatise is at once a philosophical search for the nature of the divine and at the same time an encouragement to the individual to aspire to this goal by taking his start from the beauty that is experienced in this world; for it is an image of transcendent beauty. This upward movement of the treatise reflects throughout the speech of Socrates in Plato's *Symposium* in which he recounts the exhortation of the priestess Diotima to ascend from earthly to transcendent beauty, which for Plotinus is identified with the divine.

The work is carefully structured. Plotinus commences by stating the scope of the enquiry about the nature of beauty: it will include more than physical beauty. Then, as so often, he begins with a critique of inadequate theories, in this case the widely held view that beauty is symmetry; for this theory cannot account for beauty in physical objects, let alone the beauty of incorporeal reality. As he moves on (Chapter 2) to a more positive analysis of what causes beauty, he begins his enquiry once again at the level of physical beauty and notes how we almost instinctively recognize and embrace it, whereas we are alienated by its opposite, ugliness. This phenomenon is traced back to the close affinity of our soul to intelligible being and form. As the source of form, soul, in its capacity as universal and world Soul, bestows beauty on physical objects and, in its capacity as individual soul, recognizes their beauty by comparing the form of beauty which it has in itself with the beauty in objects. Plotinus carefully attempts to account for how we recognize beauty in objects, colors, sounds and, more abstractly, in virtues and ideas, by explaining that we compare the immanent form in the object with the form in the soul. But his interest here is

not so much in providing a metaphysics of aesthetics
as in seeing exactly how it is that the beauty of physical
phenomena can provide us with a starting point for the
ascent to transcendent beauty. Yet even though the end-
point of this philosophical journey lies in a transcendent
world, it is important to recognize that Plotinus sees our
activities as rooted in the reality of the physical universe.

He now (Chapter 4) asks us to make the transition
from physical beauty to beauty at a higher and "truer"
level. "True" because now we will find ourselves at the level
of "being". Nearly all men have the means to see beauty
but not all are true "lovers of beauty," i.e. of transcendent
beauty, where beauty is no longer simply an attribute but
an essential element in the nature of true being. This
experience of beauty (Chapter 5) is important for Plotinus
because it constitutes the state of our souls and determines
our spiritual progress. The experience of the beauty of our
own soul is also a recognition of its moral and spiritual
purity. Ugliness is the exact opposite, something which
comes from outside, dilutes and obscures the beauty of
the pure soul. It is to be noted here that for Plotinus soul
and, more precisely, intellect *is* beauty. For Plato beauty
is a Form amongst other Forms; for Plotinus beauty is an
essential characteristic of intelligible reality as a whole.
This is why he can speak of virtue as a "purification" of
the soul (Chapter 6) since the true nature of the soul,
i.e. its intelligible beauty, is revealed when it is purified

of externals. This purification may also be described as
a separation of soul from the bodily since soul becomes
purer when it is no longer overwhelmed by and immersed
in the bodily. Only in this way do we become "like god,"
the final goal of the Platonic philosopher.[1] It is at this
point of the exposition that he first clearly alludes to the
metaphysical hierarchy which identifies Intellect with
Beauty but assigns to the One the role of cause of Beauty.

The framework has now been established within
which the individual must make his ascent (Chapter
7) from physical beauty, through soul, to intellect, and
finally to the One. The more familiar notions of separating ourselves and stripping off the bodily are advocated
as a practical way of making the ascent. In Chapter 8 he
turns to even more practical encouragement with a series
of images, at first negative, turning away from the world,
and then positive, embracing true being. He concludes
(Chapter 9) by referring back to the notion of inner sight.
The talk is no longer of physical beauty (see Chapter 8) but
of virtues and beautiful actions in others which act as a
stimulus. And yet even to see these we must develop our
own inner vision by turning to our inner selves to reveal
the beauty there which will enable us to recognize better
not only the virtues of others but eventually Beauty itself.
Thus, beginning with the beauty of physical objects, we

---

1   Cf. Plato, *Theaetetus* 176b1.

start to see the beauty of virtue in others, and are then stimulated to sharpen our vision by purifying our own inner vision, which in turn will lead us to the vision of Beauty itself at the level of Intellect and eventually to the vision of the Good.

In this treatise, as so often, Plotinus combines philosophical analysis with exhortation to spiritual progress. For the two are in a sense identical: the process of philosophical reflection and analysis, in this case of the nature of beauty, requires us to turn inward in reflection to discover through discursive reason the beauty that we ourselves are. The discovery of the divine and ultimately the One is a discovery of what lies at our own center and is at once the culmination of our intellectual and of our spiritual efforts.

Beauty as Symmetry

The idea that symmetry is an important aspect of beauty was fairly commonplace in Greek thought. It appears in Plato and Aristotle,[2] but was particularly espoused by the Stoics. In *Philebus* 64e7f., Plato includes symmetry as a component of the Good along with Beauty. In the *Timaeus*, right proportions are regarded as important for

---

2   For Aristotle, see *Topics* 3 116b21: "The beauty of melodies is a kind of symmetry," and *Metaphysics* 1078a36: "The chief forms of beauty are order, symmetry and definiteness."

the universe (31c) and for the equilibrium of body and soul (87c). And in *Sophist* 235e6f., symmetry (with color) is seen as an important element in art.[3] The conjunction of symmetry and color is found as Stoic teaching in Cicero's *Tusculan Disputations* IV.31, in which the health of soul is compared with beauty of the body:

> And as in the body a certain symmetrical shape of the limbs combined with a certain charm of coloring is described as beauty, so in the soul the name of beauty is given to an equipoise and consistency of beliefs and judgments, following upon virtue or comprising the true essence of virtue.[4]

> It is taken up again by Augustine (*City of God* XXII.19).

---

3   It should, however, be noted that the status of art in this passage is relatively low and the idea is introduced in order to contrast with what Plato regards as an even more inferior form of art which permits the contravention of the natural laws of proportion.

4   Et ut corporis est quaedam apta figura membrorum cum coloris quadam suavitate eaque dicitur pulchritudo, sic in animo opinionum iudiciorumque aequabilitas et constantia cum firmitate quadam et stabilitate virtutem subsequens aut virtutis vim ipsam continens pulchritudo vocatur. Cf. SVF III 278–279.

Plotinus recognizes the widespread nature of the theory when he says that it was held "by all"; but it should be noted that he immediately qualifies this remark,[5] since he is aware that Plato at least did not make it in any sense an exclusive or essential factor. So, for example, in the *Philebus* (51b3–d8) pleasure and beauty are found in simple non-composites: "[True pleasures are] those that attach to colors that we call beautiful, to figures, to most odors, to sounds . . . things like that, I maintain, are beautiful not, like most things, in a relative sense; they are always beautiful in their very nature, and they carry pleasures peculiar to themselves . . . and there are colors too which have this characteristic . . . audible sounds which are smooth and clear, and deliver a single series of pure notes, are beautiful and not relative to something else, but in themselves" (trans. R. Hackforth).

Despite, however, the emphasis in this treatise on the Platonic notion of a transcendent cause of beauty, we should be clear that Plotinus is not ruling out altogether the contribution of symmetry to beauty. So, for example, in VI.7.22 in drawing an analogy between the experience of intellectual and physical beauty he clearly suggests that symmetry constitutes a certain element of beauty in physical objects[6] and in II.9.16, 41f., symmetry

---

5   I.6.1, 21.

6   VI.7.22, 24–29 where he says that "beauty is what illuminates good proportions rather than the good proportions themselves" and

is recognized as contributing to the beauty of the physical universe, though in both cases this is rather as effect than as cause. But it remains for him inadmissible as an explanation of the cause of beauty because it runs counter to his metaphysical concept of the universe as a cosmic unity whose wholeness and unity is dependent on and is an expression of a transcendent intelligible cause. It is for this reason that he pays so much attention to disproving the cogency of the theory of symmetry. His arguments concern not only physical beauty but also the incorporeal beauty of the activities of soul. Against the former he claims that symmetry does not account for the beauty of things that are singular and without parts, although it is worth noting that the beauty of the simple also, and more significantly, applies to the intelligible world, which strictly speaking is a unity and without parts. Against the latter he argues that symmetry cannot account for the beauty of ideas and virtue, values that are ultimately of more interest to him than physical beauty. But his arguments are not entirely cogent and convincing (see Anton 1964). Some of the weak points include his failure to analyze further the possibly different meanings of simplicity in the examples he gives (gold, lightning, a musical note), or the equation of symmetry and conformity in his analysis

---

then goes on to say that "there is more light of beauty on a living face, but only a trace of it on a dead one," thus implying that there is some beauty, if only a trace (*ichnos*), on a dead person's face.

of propositions. And yet a failure to discount the case for symmetry does not disprove and need not impair the value of Plotinus' own preferred explanation of the cause of beauty, which could be accepted as a more comprehensive and explanatory theory.

The Importance and Role of Beauty

Two factors are to be noted concerning the importance of beauty in the philosophy of Plotinus. Firstly, there is the close link between beauty and love, a link which may, of course, be traced back to Plato's *Symposium* and *Phaedrus.* It first emerges in Chapter 4 as an expression of that power of attraction which is exercised by beauty, as already explained in Chapters 2 and 3. The response of love and desire is, for Plotinus, one of the most basic dynamic forces of the universe; for it is both the intrinsic power of all things to desire the Good as they turn to contemplate their causes, thus securing their own perfection, and also, in the case of the individual, the source of our ability to find our real selves by returning to our originative cause and so assimilating ourselves to god. The opening chapter of the treatise *On Love* (III.5 [50]) has ideas very similar to those in I.6, particularly in the description of the soul's initial response to beauty and ugliness in I.6.2 and 3.

> "Then everyone, of course, realizes that the affection for which we say love is re-

sponsible occurs in souls which desire to
be closely bound with beauty of some kind
and that this desire comes in one form
from the morally pure who have been assimilated to beauty itself, but in another
form also seeks to find its culmination in
the performance of some wretched act.
[15] Where each takes its rise is a proper
topic to pursue in a philosophical way in
what follows. If one were to posit as its
origin the longing for beauty itself which
is already present in men's souls, their recognition of it, kinship with it and a sub-
rational comprehension that one is to be
assimilated to it, one would, I think, hit on
the truth about its cause."

The impetus toward beauty and the Good is already
built into our nature, as an urge that is almost uncon-
sciously present, although, Plotinus recognizes, it can be
employed to perverse ends. He then goes on in this passage to speak of our instinctive rejection of what is ugly,
an idea similarly found in I.6.

A further feature of beauty which marks it as an
important concept is its being more than simply one
Form among others at the level of Intellect. In fact we
might argue that it is not a Form at all, for it is a feature

of the Intelligible World in its entirety and, in a sense, is identical with the Intelligible World. Another section from the same chapter of III.5 describes it as akin to eternity, which is not a Form but an essential property of Being.

> "And the man whose love of beauty is pure, will love beauty alone whether [40] he has recalled the archetype or not, while the man whose love is mixed with another appetite, for 'being immortal as far as is possible for a mortal,'[7] seeks what is beautiful in the 'everlasting'[8] and eternal, and as he proceeds according to nature he sows and begets in beauty, the sowing being to perpetuate himself and it is done in beauty because of the kinship of beauty and eternity. For eternity is certainly [45] akin to beauty and the eternal nature[9] is the first to be beautiful and all that proceeds from it is beautiful."

Beauty thus joins Eternity in the company of the five genera of Being, Sameness, Difference, Movement and

---

7   Plato *Symposium* 206e8.

8   Ibid.

9   I.e., Intellect.

Rest that Plotinus took from Plato's *Sophist* as defining his Intelligible World.

The Value of Physical Beauty

But is physical beauty merely a means to an end with no intrinsic value of its own, and so to be ignored or even rejected by the philosopher who has assimilated himself to the divine? There are a number of indications that Plotinus would not agree with such a view. It is not merely a ladder to be cast away after use. III.5.1 is particularly explicit about this. He has already distinguished three different kinds of love of beauty in the first half of the chapter, part of which we cited above: love of incorporeal beauty, heterosexual love, and homosexual love, which he condemns. When he returns to the topic he makes it clear that although the first kind differs from the second in that it does not find physical love and beauty sufficient, he does, nevertheless, still value it.

> "But, to return to the point, those who love beautiful bodies, but not[10] for sexual reasons, love them because they are beautiful and there are also those who have the love which is called[11] mixed, for women in order to perpetuate themselves, but if it is love for other than women they are mak-

---

10 Negative *mê* added with Ficino, Flamand, Kalligas.

11 See Plato *Laws* 837b.

ing a mistake. The first group are better, but both the first and the second are morally sound. But while the latter [60] reverence earthly beauty too and find it sufficient, the former reverence beauty in the other realm insofar as they have recalled it and yet do not disdain beauty here, given that it can be a fulfillment of beauty there and its playful expression. These then are concerned with beauty without ugliness, but there are those others who fall into ugliness even though it is on account of beauty. For the desire of good often involves the fall into evil."

But another important, and more metaphysical, point comes out in the passage from VI.7.22, which we mentioned above in speaking of symmetry.

"And are not the more lifelike statues the more beautiful ones, even if the others are better proportioned? And is not an uglier living man more beautiful than the beautiful man in a statue? Yes, because the living is more desirable; and this is because it has soul; and this is because it has more the form of good; and this means that it is somehow colored by the light of the Good."

Plotinus here notes that a statue which is more lifelike is more attractive; so too a living human who is ugly is more beautiful than the most handsome statue. The key here is *life*; and the presence of *life* is due to the presence and activity of soul, which communicates and irradiates the Good throughout the universe.[12] The implication is that the living human has a greater soul presence than a beautiful statue. In this sense Socrates is beautiful though visually ugly in the conventional sense. It is striking that Plotinus here seems to discount the ugliness of the face, an ugliness which is presumably also due to the absence of form. But Socrates' beauty still remains a physical beauty, so that we must presume that the beauty of life bestowed on the face by the soul must somehow override the other failings. We may also ask whether the beauty of the living face is quantitative in the sense that the living face manifests the presence of those form/soul powers such as movement which are not present in the statue; or is it qualitative, in that the living face manifests, for example, the inner qualities of the person (see Porphyry's account of how Plotinus could read character from a person's external appearance, *Life of Plotinus* 11).

---

12 Note, too, the introduction of the notion of *life* in I.6.7, 10.

In V.8.2, Plotinus gives us some further reflections on physical beauty. He argues that physical beauty is perceived as immanent form along with the externally expressed attributes such as size as they are taken in through the eyes. This idea is contained in the sentence (V.8.2, 27–8): "But the size is drawn in along with it, since it has become not large in bulk but 'large' in form" (*synephelketai de kai to megethos ou mega en ongkôi all' eidei genomenon mega*). This indicates that the object as perceived, although entirely constituted of forms, is perceived *as an object with physical properties* and is thus different from the ideal that is without such manifested physical properties. When he goes on in this passage to complain that we normally observe only the external manifestations of beauty without understanding the causal working of the immanent form in things, he seems to be advocating that we look only at the inner form and discount its physical expression:

> "But the beauty also in studies and ways of life and generally in souls makes clear that what is pursued is something else and that beauty does not lie in magnitude: it is truly a greater beauty than that when you see moral sense in someone and delight in it, not looking at his face—which might be ugly—but putting aside all shape and pursuing his inner beauty."

But taken in the light of the previous lines the phrase "not looking at his face" should indicate not that we should ignore his physical presence altogether, but should rather ignore the deficiencies of purely external beauty, and see the manifestations of inner beauty. From this we then progress to viewing the internal beauty alone when the immanent form is compared with the form of beauty within our own soul.

We must finally take into account the fact that Plotinus fully recognizes that we are embodied human beings and in this way always attached to and indeed dependent on the physical environment in which we live. Although the ultimate goal is complete freedom from the body and unity with Intellect and the One, Plotinus does not himself place any great weight on a purely physical disengagement, that is, a physical separation of soul and body after death. This is the import of a vivid comparison of the series of our embodied lives with the activities of an actor who enters the stage wearing different masks, or even in different plays, whilst remaining the same actor (III.2.15, 24f.). Thus the same person remains behind the changes of masks or throughout a series of reincarnations. The implication of this is that we never lose the link with a physical body and that our inner life may be promoted within the context of our physical existence. Thus our physical environment remains very much part of what we are: a complex being living at different levels. To this extent the beauty of the physical universe still remains relevant to us.

V.8 [31] On the Intelligible Beauty

Further insights into many of the ideas contained in I.6 may be obtained by reading the much later treatise "On Intelligible Beauty," which approaches some of the same subjects but from a different perspective. Whereas I.6 is primarily structured around the way in which the soul can be helped to ascend to the Intelligible through its apprehension of beauty, the later treatise is more concerned to demonstrate that beauty is something incorporeal even when found in physical objects. The treatise, in fact, forms the second part of a large tractate that was divided by Porphyry. With its first part, "On Contemplation" (III.8 [30]), its third, "That the intelligibles are not external to the Intellect and the Good" (V.5 [32]) and the fourth, "Against the Gnostics" (II.9 [33]), its grand aim is to provide a convincing account of the intelligible origin of a physical world that is worthy in its beauty and goodness of its transcendent source. The first two chapters of V.8 complement Plotinus' discussion of physical beauty in I.6. Particularly significant is their extensive comparison of artistic and natural beauty; and Plotinus here also introduces art and the role of the artist, whereas art, as opposed to beauty, is only implied in I.6. In V.8 he stresses the nature of art as imitative, not however, of any physical object, as in Plato's *Republic*, but of the ideal form. In this context he notes that the artist can even improve on nature (V.8.1, 36–37). In these respects Plotinus' view of art does not follow Plato's analysis of art in *Republic* (Book X 596a–599b) where it is criticized as being imitative of physical objects and standing at a third remove from the ideal Form behind the material object represented by the artist. Plotinus' theory echoes rather the metaphysics of the *Symposium*, where beauty is traced back to its transcendent cause, and the status of art (poetry) in the *Phaedrus*, where it is an expression of divine inspiration. Presumably Plotinus would not see a contradiction here, but would suppose that in the *Republic* Plato is considering a different context (politics/education) and, perhaps also, a different kind of art, one on a lower level. Hence possibly his refusal to have his portrait painted (Porphyry, *Life of Plotinus* 1), since this really would be at a third remove, an imitation of a particular physical reality. The sort of art that Plotinus perhaps has in mind in V.8 is the kind of idealistic sculpture represented by Phidias' statue of Zeus at Olympia, mentioned at the end of the first chapter. The ground seems already to have been prepared for such an "idealizing" trend in interpreting Plato. It appears already in Cicero (*Orator* 2.8–3.9) and in Seneca (*Letter* 65.8); in the latter as a combination of Stoic, Platonic and Aristotelian doctrines that probably goes back to

Antiochus, a Stoicizing Platonist of the first century BC. An interesting similarity of approach may also be found in the discussion by Dio of Prusa, an orator and cynic of the 2nd century AD, of Phidias' Zeus in his *Olympian Oration* (*Oration* 12), where he makes Phidias defend his representation of the god in human form and show that it does not diminish his real stature. All of this suggests that Plotinus was not out of touch with contemporary popular theories of art.

The combination of ideas from V.8 and I.6, transmitted partly through Marsilio Ficino, has had a profound influence on artistic theory from the time of the Renaissance and remains still relevant to modern debate; and this influence has ensured in no small measure the popularity of the treatise *On Beauty.* It must, however, be constantly borne in mind that, although Plotinus invested much profound thought in the nature of beauty and art, this was for him a side issue and an almost incidental consequence of his primary consideration, which was to explain the relationship of this world to its transcendent archetype and indicate the way in which we might return to our true selves and "become like god."

Note on the Text

LINE NUMBERS IN THE TRANSLATION are approximate and do not always match the original Greek text. Since the commentary follows the sequence of the English translation, there may sometimes be a slight discrepancy in the ordering.

The Greek text adopted is that of the Oxford edition (taking into account the Addenda ad Textum in vol. 3, 304–325). Deviations from the text are noted in the commentary. Each *Ennead* is referred to by Roman numerals, followed by the number of the treatise, the chapter of the treatise, and, finally, separated by a comma, the line number or numbers, e.g, V.1.3, 24–27.

It is customary to add the chronological number given by Porphyry in his *Life of Plotinus* (*Vita Plotini*), so that, for example, V.1 is designated V.1 [10]. In this series the chronological number is given only where it is of significance for Plotinus' philosophical stance. The following chart indicates the chronological order.

Chronological Order of the *Enneads*

Enn.		Enn.		Enn.		Enn.		Enn.		Enn.	
I.1	**53**	II.1	**40**	III.1	**3**	IV.1	**21**	V.1	**10**	VI.1	**42**
I.2	**19**	II.2	**14**	III.2	**47**	IV.2	**4**	V.2	**11**	VI.2	**43**
I.3	**20**	II.3	**52**	III.3	**48**	IV.3	**27**	V.3	**49**	VI.3	**44**
I.4	**46**	II.4	**12**	III.4	**15**	IV.4	**28**	V.4	**7**	VI.4	**22**
I.5	**36**	II.5	**25**	III.5	**50**	IV.5	**29**	V.5	**32**	VI.5	**23**
I.6	**1**	II.6	**17**	III.6	**26**	IV.6	**41**	V.6	**24**	VI.6	**34**
I.7	**54**	II.7	**37**	III.7	**45**	IV.7	**2**	V.7	**18**	VI.7	**38**
I.8	**51**	II.8	**35**	III.8	**30**	IV.8	**6**	V.8	**31**	VI.8	**39**
I.9	**16**	II.9	**33**	III.9	**13**	IV.9	**8**	V.9	**5**	VI.9	**9**

	Enn.		Enn.		Enn.		Enn.		Enn.		Enn.
1	I.6	**10**	V.1	**19**	I.2	**28**	IV.4	**37**	II.7	**46**	I.4
2	IV.7	**11**	V.2	**20**	I.3	**29**	IV.5	**38**	VI.7	**47**	III.2
3	III.1	**12**	II.4	**21**	IV.1	**30**	III.8	**39**	VI.8	**48**	III.3
4	IV.2	**13**	III.9	**22**	VI.4	**31**	V.8	**40**	II.1	**49**	V.3
5	V.9	**14**	II.2	**23**	VI.5	**32**	V.5	**41**	IV.6	**50**	III.5
6	IV.8	**15**	III.4	**24**	V.6	**33**	II.9	**42**	VI.1	**51**	I.8
7	V.4	**16**	I.9	**25**	II.5	**34**	VI.6	**43**	VI.2	**52**	II.3
8	IV.9	**17**	II.6	**26**	III.6	**35**	II.8	**44**	VI.3	**53**	I.1
9	VI.9	**18**	V.7	**27**	IV.3	**36**	I.5	**45**	III.7	**54**	I.7

Synopsis

Chapter 1

1–6 Beauty is found in sensibles, but also in non-sensibles.

7–16 What is the cause of sensible and non-sensible beauty? Are their causes different? For the former partake of beauty, the latter are beautiful in themselves.

16–20 What is the cause of sensible beauty? This will help us to find the cause of non-sensible beauty.

20–25 Symmetry of parts to each other and to the whole, with the addition of color.

25–30 Only the compound and the whole will be beautiful, but not the parts. But the parts must be beautiful, since what is beautiful cannot be composed of parts that are not beautiful.

30–36 In fact simple things can be beautiful. But they do no possess symmetry.

36–40 Also beauty may disappear even when the symmetry remains the same. Therefore beauty is not symmetry.

40–54 This is even more true of non-sensibles, which do not possess symmetry. Even when there is consonance between propositions, this is not beauty, for two false (ugly) propositions can be in agreement.

Chapter 2

1–7 The soul is immediately aware of beauty in physical objects before recognizing and comparing it with the form of beauty within the soul. Similarly it recoils from ugliness.

7–11 The soul rejoices at beauty because it is similar to it in nature.

11–13 Physical beauty comes from participation in form.

13–18 Ugliness is absence of form.

18–28 Form provides unity in complex objects and uniformity in simple ones.

Chapter 3

1–5 The higher part of the soul joins with the lower in recognizing beauty.

5–16 Soul compares embodied form without mass with the form already in the soul.

17–19 Embodied form also includes color caused by light, which is an incorporeal form.

19–27 And fire is the most beautiful of the four physical elements since it is very close to the incorporeal.

28–33 Musical sound, too, is caused by the embodied forms of harmony.

33–6 Physical beauty is the shadowy manifestation of embodied form.

Chapter 4

1–4 But transcendent beauty is not visible to sense-perception.

5–13 And it can be spoken of only by those who have fostered their own internal beauty.

13–17 Since transcendent beauty is true beauty it has a profound effect on the soul.

17–22 Although all men experience something of this, true lovers experience it more intensely.

Chapter 5

1–8 We must examine the experience of transcendent beauty in others and in ourselves by separating ourselves from the physical body.

8–16 These beauties will be found to be completely incorporeal and properties of the soul presided over by intellect.

16–20 But what makes all these things beautiful? They are identical with being.

21–25 It will help us further to identify this beauty if we understand what ugliness is.

25–46 Ugliness in the soul is something added from outside which drags it away from itself to the external and corporeal.

46–58 We must remove this accretion to regain our original purity and beauty.

Chapter 6

1–13 We must, like the initiates purified in mystery rites, separate ourselves from the body and physical things.

13–21 The soul then becomes form and beautiful and good as it approaches intellect and becomes like God.

21–6 Moreover, Beauty is identical with true being, ugliness with matter and evil.

26–32 Beauty and the Good come first, followed by Intellect which is beautiful, then soul made beautiful by Intellect, then actions, ways of life, and bodies made beautiful by soul.

Chapter 7

1–12 The soul desires the Good and beautiful by removing the layers acquired during descent, like initiates removing their garments, until it sees the good through its own self; this is the divine which is the cause of life, being, and thought.

12–18 Attaining this has a profound impact on the soul.

18– 21 It leads us to despise lower kinds of beauty and love.

21–30 For these come from outside and are derivative, but true beauty is self-contained and makes its lovers beautiful and loveable.

30–33 It is the highest goal and brings the greatest happiness.

34–39 And misfortune consists not in the failure to acquire worldly beauty and power but in not reaching the vision of true beauty.

Chapter 8

1–3 How do we achieve this beauty?

3–8 We must turn away from physical beauties, which are mere shadows, and turn our gaze inward to their archetypes.

8–16 If we behave like Narcissus, who mistook his image for his real self, we will live in a world of shadows both now and after our death.

16–21 We must leave behind the beauty of Circe and Calypso to return to our homeland.

22–7 We must abandon all physical experiences and employ the inner vision which all have, but few use.

Chapter 9

1–6 Your inner vision must be acclimatized by looking at the virtuous activities and then the souls of good men.

6–15 You must then attend to your own virtues and make your internal statue beautiful until you become virtuous and beautiful within.

15–34 When you have fully identified yourself with this inner perfection you no longer need a guide, but like sees like and one becomes godlike and beautiful in order to see god and beauty.

34–40 You ascend first to Beauty and Intellect and then to the Good (the One).

40–43 It is the primal beauty but, if we make distinctions in the transcendent world, we will say that Intellect is beauty and the Good is beyond beauty and is its cause.

Translation of
Plotinus Ennead *I.6*

On Beauty

1. Beauty is found for the most part in sight, but it is found also in hearing, both in the composition of words, as well as being found in music; indeed in all aspects of music, for both melody and rhythm are beautiful. And for those proceeding upward from sense perception there are | beautiful ways of life, actions, dispositions and items 5 of knowledge as well as the beauty of the virtues. And if there is any beauty beyond even these, it will itself make it manifest.

Then what is it that has made us imagine bodies to be beautiful and our hearing to assent to sounds as being beautiful? And how can all the things that are directly concerned with soul be beautiful? And is | everything 10 [beautiful] by one and the same beauty? Or is beauty one thing in the body and something else in another

thing? And what could these or this thing be? For some things, for example bodies, are not beautiful from their own underlying substances but by participation, whilst others are beauties themselves, such as the nature of virtue. For the same bodies sometimes appear beautiful
15 and sometimes not, | since their being bodies is different from their being beautiful. What then is this that is present to bodies? For our enquiry must begin with this. What is it that stirs the gaze of those who look and turns them toward itself, draws them and makes them delight
20 in what they see? For if we find this, | we would probably see the rest too, "using it as a stepping stone."

It is said by virtually all that symmetry of the parts to each other and to the whole with the addition of fine color is the cause of visual beauty, and that for visible things and in general all other things being beautiful is being
25 symmetrical and | measured. For those who hold this view nothing simple but only a compound is of necessity beautiful. And for them the whole will be beautiful, while the parts will not have their beauty from themselves, but as contributing to make the whole beautiful. And yet if the whole is beautiful the parts too must be beautiful; for it
30 certainly must not be made up of | ugly parts, but beauty must have taken hold of all the parts. And for them colors that are beautiful including, for example, the light of the sun, must be excluded from being beautiful, since they are simple and so do not have beauty from symmetry.

Then how is gold, too, beautiful? And how does anyone find lightning and stars at night beautiful to behold? In the case of sounds, too, | the simple will rule itself out   35 for the same reasons; and yet frequently each of the notes in a composition, which is beautiful as a whole, is also itself beautiful.

But in fact when the same face appears at one time to be beautiful, at another time not, whilst the symmetry remains identical, surely one must say that being beautiful is something other than and beyond proportion, and | that proportion is beautiful because of something else.   40

But if, when they go on to ways of life and arguments that are beautiful, they identify symmetry as the cause in their case as well, what could be termed symmetry in beautiful ways of life, laws, studies or items of knowledge? How could propositions be symmetrical | with each other?   45 If [their answer is] that they are concordant, there is both concordance and agreement in bad ones too; for "prudence is silliness" and "justice is noble stupidity" are concordant, harmonious and agree with each other. Every kind of virtue is beauty of soul and beauty which is | more true   50 than those we have already mentioned. But how are they symmetrical? For they are symmetrical neither as quantities nor as number. And since soul consists of numerous parts, in what ratio is the composition or mixture of the parts or of the propositions [to be found]? Finally what would be the beauty of intellect when isolated on its own?

2. Then we should go back to the beginning and state what really is the starting point of beauty in bodies.

Well, it is something which becomes perceptible at even the first glance, which the soul expresses as if it understood it, accepts when it recognizes it and fits, as it

5   were, to itself. | But when the soul directs its sight to something ugly "it shrinks back," disowns it and recoils from it, without harmonizing with it but becoming estranged. We claim, in fact, that the soul, since it is in its nature what it is and is close to the more superior reality among real beings, rejoices at whatever it sees that is akin to it or is

10   a trace of what is akin to it, is thrilled, | refers it to itself and recalls its own self and its own contents. What then is the likeness of beautiful things in this world to those in the intelligible realm? For if there is a likeness we must say that they are alike.

Yet how are things there and things here both beautiful?

We affirm that things here are beautiful by participation in form. For everything that is formless but capable of receiving shape and form, as long as it is without a

15   share of | reason principle and form, is ugly and outside divine reason principle. And this is complete ugliness. And what is not mastered by shape and reason principle, since its matter is not capable of supporting complete shaping by the form, is also ugly. And so the form draws near and arranges together the thing that is going to

become composed as one from many parts, | guides it to 20
become a single complete entity and makes it one by the
agreement [of its parts], since the form itself was one and
what is formed must also be one as far as this is possible
for something that is composed of many parts. Beauty
is, then, established upon it once it has been brought
together in unity and it gives itself to both parts and
wholes. But when it takes hold of something that is one
and composed of parts that are alike, | it gives the same 25
form to the whole [as to the parts], for example, in the
former case when craftsmanship gives beauty to a whole
house together with its parts, but in the latter when a
certain nature gives beauty to a single stone. It is in this
way, in fact, that the beautiful body comes into being—by
sharing in the reason principle, which has come from the
divine [forms].

3. Now the power that is assigned to this task gets
to know beauty, and nothing is more effective in judging
what belongs to it, whenever the rest of the soul joins with
it in judging; and perhaps this very power, too, makes a
statement by fitting [what it sees] with the form in it and
using it in its judgment like | a ruler for a straight line.   5

But how does the form in body agree with that which
is prior to body? And how does the builder state that the
external house is beautiful by comparing it with the form
of house within him?

Surely it is because the external house, if you were to separate off the stones, is the internal form divided by the external mass of matter, something which is part-
10 less though appearing in multiplicity. And so whenever | sense perception sees that the form in bodies has bound and mastered the nature which is opposed to it which is shapeless, and sees shape riding magnificently on other shapes, it draws close together the disparate and refers it back and leads it, by now partless, within, and then gives
15 it to what is within as in agreement, | fitting and dear to it, just as when a welcome trace of virtue in a young man manifests itself to a good man and is in agreement with the truth within him.

And the simple beauty of color shapes and masters the darkness of matter by the presence of incorporeal light, which is reason principle and form. And this is why fire
20 itself is beautiful beyond other bodies, | because it has the rank of form as compared with the other elements, being above them in position and the most subtle of all other bodies, since it is close to the incorporeal and it alone does not receive the others, whereas the others receive it. For they are warmed but it is not chilled; and it has color in a
25 primary way while the others | take the form of color from it. So it shines and gleams as though it were a form. But the fire which does not master and whose light is fading is no longer beautiful, since it would not be participating in the complete form of color.

And the hidden harmonies in musical sounds make the ones that are manifest and by so doing make the soul | become aware of beauty, by displaying the same thing 30 in a different [medium]. And it is a feature of perceptible harmonies to be measurable numerically, not in any kind of formula but the sort that is capable of serving the production of form in its task of mastering.

So much for the beauties of sense experience, which are images and shadows which, as it were, | run forth and 35 enter matter and adorn it; and thrill us too when they are made manifest.

4. But as for the beauties beyond, which it is not given to sense-perception to see but which soul sees and states without the organs of perception, these we must view by ascending and leaving sense-perception to wait below. And just as in the case of the beauties of sense-perception it was not possible | for those who, like men 5 blind from birth, had not seen them or grasped them as beauties, to make statements about them, in the same way it is not possible for those who have not absorbed the beauty of good practices, items of knowledge and other such things to speak about the beauty of good practices, | nor for those who have not even imagined how beauti- 10 ful is "the face of justice" and temperance to speak about the "splendor" of virtue: "Neither Evening nor Morning Star are so beautiful."

But they must be men seeing by that with which the soul sees such things and, when they see, they must be delighted, be struck and thrilled much more than by those 15 earlier beauties, since they are | now grasping true beauties. For these must be the affections which occur with whatever is beautiful, wonder, shock of delight, yearning, love and a thrill accompanied with delight. It is possible to have these experiences and souls do have them; and, in the case of beauties not perceived by the senses all souls experience them to an extent, but more especially 20 so those more in love with these things, | just as in the case of bodies all men see them, but are not smitten to the same degree, but there are those who are more smitten who are the ones who are also said to be in love.

5. Then we must question those who are also lovers of non-sensible beautiful things: what do you experience when it comes to what we call beautiful ways of life, beautiful manners, temperate moral behavior and, in general, virtuous activities and dispositions and the beauty of 5 souls? | And what is your experience when it is yourselves you see, beautiful in your inner lives? And how are you aroused and stirred and yearn to be in the company of your inner selves when you have gathered yourselves from your bodies? For these are the things that those who are lovers in the real sense experience.

But what is the focal point of these experiences? It is 10 not shape, not color, | not size of any kind, but soul is the

focal point, which is itself "without color" but possesses
temperance without color and the "splendor" of the other
virtues. [This is what you experience] whenever you see
in yourself, or observe in another, greatness of soul, a just
character, pure temperance, courage with its manly visage,
| dignity and respect hovering over them in a disposition   15
which is steadfast, unperturbed and unfazed; and shining
over all of these the godlike intellect. We admire and love
these things, but how is it that we call them beautiful?

It is, of course, because they exist and are made
manifest and the one who has seen them can say nothing
other than that they are what really exists.

What does | "really exists" mean?   20

That they are beautiful things.

But reason still wants to know what it is in what really
exists that has made the soul loveable. What is it that is
pre-eminent over all the virtues like a light?

Would you care, then, to take the opposite of beauty,
the ugliness that comes about in soul, and compare them?
For perhaps it would help us to find what we are looking
for if it was made clear | what ugliness is and why. Then   25
suppose a soul to be ugly, ill-disciplined and unjust, full
of cravings and all kinds of disturbance, in the midst of
fears because of cowardice, and of jealousies because of
petty-mindedness, thinking of everything in so far as it
thinks of them at all, as mortal and lowly, twisted in every
respect, in love with pleasures that are impure, | living   30

a life of pure bodily sensations and taking ugliness as a delight. Aren't we then to say that this very ugliness was added to it as a sort of "beauty" brought in from outside, something which caused it harm and made it impure and "jumbled up" with a great deal of evil, no longer in pos-
35 session of a life and perception | that is pure, but mixed with a great deal of death and leading a life that is dimmed because of the admixture of evil, seeing no longer what a soul ought to see and no longer allowing itself to abide in itself since it is continually being dragged toward what is outside and beneath it and in darkness? Since it really is, I
40 think, impure and carried | and drawn on all sides toward the things that impinge on sense-perception, and since it has a large amount of what is body mixed in with it, and consorts with much that is material and has taken into itself a form that is different from itself, it has changed by a mixture which has made it worse. It is just as if someone who has sunk into mud and mire no longer displays the
45 beauty he once had, | but there can be seen only what he has wiped onto himself from the mud and mire. This man's ugliness has come to him by the addition of what is alien and his task, if he is going to be beautiful again, is, by washing and purifying himself, to be what he was before. We would then be right to say that a soul is ugly by mixture, mingling and inclination toward body and
50 matter. | And this is ugliness for a soul, not to be pure or unadulterated like gold, but filled out with what is

earthy; if he manages to cast this off, the gold is left and it is beautiful, isolated from everything else, consorting with itself alone. The soul too, in the same way, when it has been isolated from the cravings | which it possesses   55 as a result of its over-familiarity with the body and has been relieved of the other affections and purified from what it has acquired in its embodied state, now that it abides alone, has put aside entirely the ugliness which comes from the other nature.

6. For in fact, as ancient tradition has it, temperance, courage and every virtue is a purification, and so also is wisdom itself. And so the mystery rites, too, correctly intimate that the man who has not been purified will lie in mire even when he goes to Hades | because what   5 is impure is enamored of mud by reason of its badness, just as pigs, too, since they are unclean in body, enjoy that kind of thing. For what else could true temperance really be than not being on familiar terms with the pleasures of the body, but fleeing them as impure and inappropriate to the man who is pure? And courage is the absence of the fear of death. And this, death, is the separation | of soul   10 from body. But the man who loves to be alone does not fear this. In fact greatness of soul is despising the things of this world. And wisdom is intellection which turns away from what is beneath and leads the soul to what is above.

And so the soul once purified becomes form and reason principle, completely bodiless, intellective and

15 belonging entirely to the | divine, whence flows beauty and all the kind of things related to it. So when soul is led up to intellect it is all the more beautiful. Intellect and the things from it are beauty for the soul, its very own and not another's beauty, because it is then that it really is just soul. Thus it is also correct to say that for the soul to
20 become something good and beautiful is for it | to become like god, for from him come beauty and the rest of reality. Or rather, beautifulness is true being and ugliness is the other nature. And this is identical with the primary evil, so that in the case of god what is beautiful and good is the same and so is the good and beautifulness.

25 And so we must enquire after beauty and | goodness, ugliness and evil, in the same way. And we must first posit beautifulness, which is also the good. Directly from this is intellect, which is the beautiful; and soul is something beautiful by the agency of intellect. And the rest of things in sequence, beauties in actions as well as in ways of life, are beautiful from soul shaping them. And so too bod-
30 ies, as many as are described as beautiful, | soul makes beautiful in turn. For since soul is something divine and a sort of portion of beauty, everything it can grasp and master it makes beautiful as far as they can share in it.

7. So we must make our ascent once more to the good, which every soul desires. Anyone who has seen it knows what I mean, when I say that it is beautiful. For it is desired as good and this desire is directed to what is good; but

attaining it is for those who make the ascent to what is
above, | have turned to it and divested themselves of the 5
garments they put on in their descent, just as for those
who climb the temple steps into the holy of holies there
are purifications, divesting of their previous garments
and the naked ascent, until one passes by in the ascent
all that is alien to the divine and sees by means of oneself
alone the divine alone, unadulterated, simple, pure; from
it all depend and to it everything looks | and is, lives and 10
thinks. For it is the cause of life, intellect and existence.
Then if anyone sees this, what feelings of love, what yearn-
ings would he have, in his desire to be intimately mingled
with it, with what feelings of enjoyment will he be struck?
For the man who has not yet seen it has | the desire for it 15
as something good, but he who has seen it is astounded
at its beauty, is filled with wondrous enjoyment, is struck
without experiencing harm, and comes to love true love
and intense yearning, while laughing at other kinds of love
and despising what he previously thought was beautiful. It
is similar to what those experience who have encountered
the forms of gods | or spirits and can no longer entertain 20
the beauties of other bodies in the same way. "What then
are we to think, if someone should behold the beautiful
itself," pure in itself, "full, not of flesh," not of body, not on
earth nor in heaven, so that it can be pure? For all these
things are brought in from outside and are mingled in and
| are not primary, but derived from the beautiful itself. 25

Then if one were to see that which supplies everything
[with beauty], gives while remaining in itself and does not
receive anything into itself, and if one were to abide in the
contemplation of such beauty, enjoy it and be made like
it, what need of further beauty would there be? For this
very beauty, since it is Beauty itself in the highest degree
30   and the primary Beauty, makes | its lovers beautiful and
renders them loveable. Indeed the contest for this prize is
the greatest and the "ultimate that is posed to our souls"
and for it the greatest "endeavor" too, that we do not go
without a share in the most noble vision; the man who
attains it is blessed in having seen that "blessed sight,"
he who does not attain it is truly unfortunate. For it is
not the man who has failed in attaining beautiful colors
35   or bodies, | or power and office, or rule over an empire,
who is unfortunate, but he who has not attained that for
whose attainment alone he ought to forego kingship and
rule over the whole earth and sea and sky, so long as by
abandoning and despising these he can turn to it and see it.

8. What then is the way? What contrivance? How
will anyone behold the "inconceivable Beauty," which
remains, as it were, within the sacred temples and does
not come forth into the outside so that a profane person
too could see it? Let him who is able leave outside the
5   sight | of his eyes and not turn to the bodily splendors
which he saw before but proceed and follow within. For
when he has seen bodily beauties he must not rush up to

them, but realizing that they are images and traces and
shadows he must flee to that whose images they are. For
anyone who runs up to the image wanting to grasp it as
though it was real, like the man who wanted to grasp his
| beautiful reflection floating on the surface of the water, 10
but sank into the stream to be seen no more, as told in
the story which has, I think, a hidden meaning, he too
since he clings to beautiful bodies without letting them
go, will in the same way sink, not in body but in soul, into
the darkness and depths which bring no joy to intellect,
where, | remaining blind in Hades, he will consort with 15
shadows both in this life and the next. "Let us flee then
to our beloved homeland" would be the sounder advice
one might give.

What then is our escape and how will we achieve it?

We will set sail as did Odysseus from the sorceress
Circe or from Calypso, as [Homer] says—with a hidden
meaning, I think: he did not want to stay though he had | 20
pleasures of sight and enjoyed much beauty of the senses.
Yet our homeland is there whence we came and there too
is our father.

What is our journey to be, what our escape?

It is not one that we may accomplish on foot; for the
feet bring us everywhere in this world from one land to
another. Nor is it one you must make by preparing some
coach or ship. You must let all | these things go and not 25
look to them, but like one shutting his eyes, you must

change to another way of seeing and arouse it, one which everyone possesses but few make use of.

9. What then does that inner sight see?

When newly stimulated it is unable to see the brightness at all. So one must accustom the soul itself firstly to look at beautiful ways of life, then at beautiful achieve-
5 ments, not those which the arts produce, | but ones produced by those who are called good men. Next look at the souls of those who produce these beautiful achievements.

How will you see the kind of beauty the good soul has?

Go back to yourself and see. And if you do not yet see yourself as beautiful, just as the sculptor of a statue which has to become beautiful removes one piece here,
10 files another, makes this part smooth, that | clean-cut, until he has revealed a face that is beautiful on his statue, so do you too remove what is excessive and align what is distorted, lighten what is dark and make it bright, and never cease "working on" your "statue" until the godlike splendor of virtue shines forth on you, until you can see
15 | "temperance established on its sacred pedestal."

If you have become this, have seen it and kept your own company in purity and have within nothing else mingled in with it, but are yourself in your entirety true light alone, a light not measured in size or restricted and
20 reduced by shape | or increased by boundlessness to become large, but in every respect unmeasured, since it is greater than all measure and superior to all quantity—if

you see yourself become this, now that you have become vision, take heart about yourself and now that you have made the ascent and no longer have need of someone to point out the way, strain your eyes and see. For this | alone is the eye that sees the great Beauty. But anyone 25 who approaches the vision bleary eyed with wickedness, uncleansed or weak, unable through cowardice to look at this great brightness, sees nothing, even if someone else points out what is present and able to be seen. For one must cast one's gaze on the vision | after making what sees 30 akin to what is seen. For an eye could never see the sun if it had not first become sun-like, nor could a soul see the beautiful if it has not become beautiful. Then a man must first become all godlike and all beautiful if he is going to behold god and beauty. For he will first come to intellect in his ascent | and there he will know the forms, all of them 35 beautiful, and he will say that this is Beauty, the Ideas. For everything is beautiful by these, the progeny of intellect and being. And we call what is beyond this the nature of the Good, which has the beautiful projected before it. So in a rough sense it is the primal | beauty, but, if one 40 makes distinctions in the intelligible world, one will say that intelligible beauty is the place of the forms, and the Good is what is beyond beauty, its "source and origin." Or one will put the Good and beauty on the same level. In any case beauty is in the transcendent world.

Commentary

Chapter 1

1, 1–20 Right from the beginning it is clear that Plotinus is concerned with more than physical beauty, which is to be put on the lowest level of beauty. At this level beauty is not identical with the essence of the thing itself. Objects of physical beauty may be beautiful at one moment but not at the next, whereas beauty at the highest level is constant and one with that which is beautiful. Nevertheless, Plotinus begins his enquiry at the level of physical beauty. But this is more than a purely intellectual enquiry, for beauty engages and stirs us. We are clearly put into the context of moral and spiritual improvement and ascent as described in Plato's *Symposium* (20).

In emphasizing beauty in sight and hearing Plotinus may have in mind Plato's *Greater Hippias* 297e–298a (Socrates goes on to mention "ways of life and laws" [298b2]). In *Topics* 146a21–32, Aristotle gives sight and sound as examples when discussing contraries.

This opening paragraph also sets out a number of questions that are answered in the course of the treatise. There are four main questions:

1. Is there beauty beyond the virtues? (6): this is answered in 6, 26–32 with the mention of beauty at the level of Intellect and the One.

2. What is the cause of our perception of physical beauty? (7–8): this is answered in Chapters 2 and 3 with the discussion of form in objects.

3. How can things connected with soul (incorporeals) be beautiful? (9): this is answered in Chapter 4 and particularly in Chapter 5 with the identification of what is beautiful with being.

4. To the series of related questions (Is there one cause of beauty? Is there a different cause of beauty in bodies and incorporeals? What is the cause of beauty in bodies? [10–16]) the complex response, that the cause is Form but at different levels, emerges gradually as the analysis presented in the treatise unfolds.

1, 3 A similar pair of components of music, designated as "all music," is found in V.9.11, 9: rhythm and harmony (*harmonia*), the latter perhaps corresponding to "melody."

1, 5–6 *ways of life ... knowledge*: The list is partly borrowed from Plato (for "ways of life and items of knowledge" see *Symposium* 210c6). "Dispositions" (*hexeis*) is an Aristotelian ethical term. The list may be regarded as presenting an ascending order from the more physical.

1, 12–3 *underlying substances*: Another example of an Aristotelian term (*hypokeimenon*) used together with the notion of "participation" (*methexis*) which is developed from Plato's description of particulars as participating in form (e.g., *Parmenides* 132d3).

1, 13 Plotinus uses the noun "beauties" (*kallê*) here rather than the noun formed from the neuter plural (*kala*) of the adjectival form (*kalos*), because, as we will see later in the treatise (5, 19–20), virtues at the intellectual level do not "share" in beauty as an attribute, but have it as an essential element of their reality.

1, 18 *turns them towards*: The idea of turning inward and upward (*epistrophe*) is one of Plotinus' key metaphysical concepts. Each level of reality is not only generated by its prior but also has its own power of turning upward to contemplate its cause and in so doing to perfect itself.

The hypostases do this always, but the individual soul only intermittently and with great effort. But its spiritual excellence depends on this effort.

1, 20 Plato, *Symposium* 211c3.

1, 21–54 The rest of the chapter is taken up with a critique of the popular and widespread theory that closely connects symmetry and beauty. But though critical of this idea he does not reject it entirely but only as inadequate as an explanation of beauty. For Plotinus, if symmetry is sometimes a component of beauty, it is an effect rather than a cause. (See Introduction, pages 21–22.)

1, 34 "stars": Plotinus may be thinking of the planet Venus, mentioned in a quotation from Euripides cited in Chapter 4, 11–12. Venus, the evening and morning star, appears at first alone in the sky.

Plotinus leaves open the nature of "simplicity" in the examples he gives here. Is it the same in each case? In gold it is a question of homogeneity; in the case of a musical note that it is cut off and separated from other notes. But it may still be complex in itself (consisting of pitch, timbre, tone); or perhaps he is thinking of a single note as opposed to a chord, and may have had in mind Plato, *Philebus* 51b–d (cited above, Introduction, page 21), which refers to the pleasure and beauty of simple things like colors and musical notes, where it is clear that Plato is thinking not of an isolated note but an identical note played by both singer and accompanist; see also *Laws* VII 812d, where Plato recommends in musical education the avoidance of all complications such as variation in pitch and interval between singer and cithara accompanist. In the case of lightning and stars it is not altogether clear to what Plotinus is referring. A stroke of lightning might be conceived to be a simple thing in view of its happening in an instant and therefore apparently without measure of time and space. A star might be considered as a simple thing compared with the complex system of stars in which it is embedded. But all of these raise questions about what it means for a physical entity to be simple—an enquiry made all the more complex by modern atomic theory.

1, 43 *laws, studies*: For "laws" see Plato, *Symposium* 210c34; "studies" 211c6−8.

1, 44−49 Plotinus denies that propositions can have symmetry and then entertains the possible rejoinder that symmetry in propositions could be understood as their concordance or agreement. He then takes two propositions from Plato (*Republic* 560d2−3; 348c11−12; *Gorgias* 491e2, with both of which, of course, Plato does not agree) and claims that they are concordant with each other (in that they do not contradict each other). If these are "bad" propositions, in the sense of being untrue and unacceptable, they can hardly be termed "beautiful." Then their "symmetry" would not be a cause of beauty. See Anton 1964 for a detailed criticism of the cogency of Plotinus' arguments here and particularly of his sleight of hand in equating "symmetry" with "concordance."

1, 51   *parts*: The term "parts" is applied frequently by Platonists to the soul but, of course, not in the physical sense. Plotinus would have in mind not only the Platonic tripartite soul (*Republic* 435a–444e) but also the Aristotelian enumeration of soul faculties which Plotinus incorporated into his own thought: growth, sensation, and reason. On Plotinus' amalgamation of Platonic and Aristotelian elements in his psychology, see Blumenthal (1971, 1972).

Chapter 2

Plotinus now explains the way in which the active engagement with beauty that he refers to in the previous chapter takes place at the very lowest level, the encounter with physical beauty. This explanation involves a number of complex philosophical factors Plotinus explores in other treatises: the way in which form relates to matter (II.5 and 6); the nature of soul and theory of perception (IV.1–9); and matter and evil (I.8; II.4).

2, 1–10 Our soul is said to grasp beauty because it recognizes in it a "likeness" with itself, since the soul is something beautiful. This notion of the soul's beauty may be traced back to Plato, for example, in *Republic* 611d we have the image of the sea-god Glaucus, the beauty of whose soul is obscured by the accretions of the physical body expressed by the barnacles and seaweed that have attached themselves to him. More precisely the idea invokes the nature of soul as possessor of the forms, or rather the *logoi* or images of the forms (see 10 *its own contents*). On the other hand, our soul recoils from ugliness which is seen as the opposite of beauty and the absence of form.

2, 2–4 The apprehension of beauty here seems to be a preliminary stage to that described at the beginning of the next chapter. This immediate awareness of beauty represents for Plotinus, as explained in the introduction, an important insight into the way in which we begin to access the intelligible world. We may note the cognitive processes involved "expressing" (*legei*), "understanding" (*sunesis*), "recognition" (*epignosis*) and "fitting" (*harmozein*) and that "understanding" and "fitting" are qualified ("as if," "as it were"). This should be compared with the description at the beginning of the next chapter of the process which seems to be taking place at, or at least involving, a higher level of soul when the rest of the soul (i.e., other than the lower faculty of immediate perception) is said to be involved in making judgments and the forms within the soul are explicitly employed. This state of primary awareness is described in similar terms in III.5.1, 17f. For *epignosis* see also II.9.16, 45 ; IV.4.5, 16 and V.3.2, 11f.

That some kind of judgment (*krisis*) is involved even at this stage is implied by the statement in the following chapter (3) that the rest of the soul "joins with it in judging" (*sunepikrinêi*). For Plotinus all perceptions involve some form of judgment from the very moment that a sensory affection is detected. (See Emilsson 1988, 121–125).

2, 3 *expresses*: In III.5, he describes the "understanding" the soul has of its own "likeness [to what is perceived]" in this primary awareness of beauty as *alogos*. But this need not contradict "expresses" (*legei*) here, since *alogos* refers to the inchoate and not fully rationalized act of perception which does, nevertheless, make an affirmation of some kind. See Emilsson 1988, 125 who refers to VI.3.18, 7–11 where in distinguishing colors Plotinus says, "it is either sense-perception or intellect which *says* that they are different, and they will not give a reason (*logos*), sense-perception because the reason (*logos*) does not belong to it, but only giving different indications . . ." Here we have the same apparent paradox of denial of *logos* and "saying."

2, 5 *"it shrinks back"*: Plato, *Symposium* 206d6. Plato speaks in this passage (206d1–7) of the antipathy of the divine (and soul) to ugliness.

2, 6 *becoming estranged*: See also I.6.6, 17 and III.6.1, 21 in both cases coupled with *oikeiosis* (appropriation). Behind these expressions lies the Stoic idea that the individual instinctively affirms and accepts what is according to his nature whilst rejecting what is alien. See Long and Sedley (1987) I.346–54. But Plotinus makes his own modifications of the Stoic doctrine: 1. Whilst accepting that the Good is *oikeion* to the soul (VI.5.1, 18), he qualifies this (VI.7.27) to affirm that it is *oikeion* because it is good, but one may not say that it is good because it is *oikeion*. This non-reciprocal affirmation ensures the transcendence at each level of the object for which one strives. In the same sense each level of reality is akin to what is above it but what is above is not akin, in the same sense, to what is beneath it. 2. Whilst allowing that soul and intellect may have a natural propensity to belong to or turn to themselves, this cannot be said of the Good or the One which does not turn to itself but is a good only to others (VI.7.41, 28–9).

2, 7 *the soul . . . real beings*: The nature of soul is discussed extensively in the treatises of *Ennead* IV. In the context of this treatise there are several features of soul which it is important to understand:

1. The primary function of soul is to give life to body and thus it is never fully separate from body. This is important in the context of this treatise because it serves the causal continuity of beauty from the intelligible to the physical level and the reverse movement of perception of beauty from the physical to the intelligible. It thus helps to bridge the transition from corporeal to incorporeal.

2. Its difference from intellect, which stands at an ontologically higher level. Thus soul and intellect represent separate levels of the ascent to the Beautiful which is the subject of this treatise.

3. That soul in its rational capacity contains images (*logoi*) of the Forms present primarily in Intellect. They function as part of the way in which beauty is recognized at different levels.

the more superior reality among real beings: by "the more superior reality" he here means intellect. "Real beings" here is used in the more generic sense of incorporeal realities which includes both soul and intellect. Elsewhere "beings" may be used more strictly of Intellect seen as the realm of forms which are real beings in the full sense.

2, 9 *what is akin to* it: See Plato, *Phaedo* 79d3 for the kinship of soul to the divine. Relevant also here is the traditional doctrine, held also by Plato, that like is perceived by like (see *Timaeus* 37a–c and Aristotle's interpretation of this in *On the Soul* 404b17 and 405b15–19). See Plotinus I.8.1, 8; II.4.10, 3.

2, 11–28 The rest of the chapter responds to the question how the beauty in physical objects relates to the beauty of incorporeals. The solution involves an explication of the relationship of form to matter. Here Plotinus goes well beyond the relatively simple Platonic concept of participation, that multiple physical objects can share in a single transcendent form, to present a more dynamic notion of the way in which form imposes itself on matter.

2, 14–16 These lines refer to matter which for Plotinus is without any form; nor is it simply some thing without or deprived of form, but is privation itself. For this reason it is *complete ugliness.* The following lines refer to bodies, that is, combinations of matter and some form—*not capable of supporting complete shaping by the form*; and these too are ugly insofar as they only partially share in form. Presumably such bodies may also manifest some aspects of beauty in so far as they have some share in form. For Plotinus prime matter (that is matter without any attributes conferred by form) is considered to be not only complete ugliness but also evil and the cause of evil, not of course moral evil which is the responsibility of the individual, but of any lack of order or beauty in the universe. But the evil presented by matter is of prime concern for the individual because it provides the environment that so easily overwhelms the soul if it does not resist it, and moral failure is precisely our submission to its allure.

2, 15 *reason principle and form*: The words "shape" (*morphe*), form (*eidos*), and "reason principle" (*logos*) have each a slightly different nuance. Shape has more the connotation of what is manifest or perceptible, "form" in the present context is the standard Platonic notion of Form, whether viewed as immanent or transcendent, while *logos* has a wide range of meanings, including "reason," "argument," "expression." In this context, as so often, it has a meaning

similar to that of "form," but brings with it a hierarchi-
cal implication of successive levels or expressions of
form as they unfold from the highest level (divine reason
principles in Intellect) to the lowest embodied instance.
I have added the description "reason" to indicate the
rational and ordered, a property which is implied by the
root word *legein* (to say): a *logos* is the expressed product
of rational thought. Form, on the other hand, suggests
more the notion of image. It should be emphasized that all
three, and particularly "form" and "reason principle," are
conceived as active powers and entities in their own right.

2, 19f. We should note here the importance of unity in
the transmission of beauty through form. Ultimately the
One, as cause of all, is the cause of unity and coherence.
We would also expect this, then, to be a factor in the
discussion, briefly touched on at the end of this treatise,
as to whether Intellect or the One is to be identified
with beauty itself. For all Neoplatonists degrees of unity
are to be identified with degrees of reality or being. See
Ennead VI.9.1, lines 1 and 14–17: "It is by the One that
all beings are beings . . . And there is health when the
body is brought together into one order, and beauty when
the nature of the one holds the parts together; and the
soul has virtue when it is unified into one thing and one
agreement"; See Porphyry, *Sententiae* 11: "Incorporeal
realities, in the process of descent, undergo fragmentation

and multiplication, to the point of forming individual things, by reason of diminution of power; while on the other hand, in the process of ascent, they are brought to unity and converge towards togetherness, by reason of superabundance of power"; Proclus, *Elements of Theology*, prop. 13: "Every good tends to unify what participates in it; and all unification is a good."

2, 24–27 Plotinus often distinguishes between natural and man-made objects (See V.8.1–2). Presumably Plotinus would recognize that some natural things are also complex, for example the human body. Would he also recognize simple man-made objects, for example glass? Here, however, his primary concern is to note that beauty brings unity both to complex things made up of different parts and to simple things, any part of which is qualitatively the same as the whole, for instance gold or as here a stone. Simple objects have already been mentioned in the argument in Chapter 1, that beauty does not consist in symmetry.

Chapter 3

The simple awareness of beauty is taken further. The soul now invoking its higher powers acquires a better grasp of beauty by comparing its sense-impressions with the forms it already has within it from intellect. It is for this reason that he now goes into further detail about the relationship of the form within soul (and transcendent form in intellect) with the form-representation which sense-perception provides; and so there is further consideration of the relationship of embodied and transcendent form and the way in which the former is experienced by the soul. The discussion of embodied form then extends beyond external shape to include color which is treated separately as a different manifestation of form, and also sound. The addition of sound (28–31) recalls the categories of sight and hearing introduced as the constituents of physical beauty at the beginning of Chapter 1.

3, **1** Note the emphasis on "getting to know" (*ginôskei*) which in Greek is the first word of the sentence.

3, 1–5 *the power that is assigned to this task* is that aspect
of the soul whose operations are described in Chapter 2,
but Plotinus implies here that its powers of discernment
are augmented when it works together with the higher
faculties of the soul which are indicated by the phrase
the rest of the soul. The "rest of the soul" may be identified
with the more complex operations that are the sphere of
discursive reason. A similar division may be seen in V.3.3,
1–2 where sense-perception is said to "give its impression
(*tupos*) of a sense-object to discursive reason (*dianoia*)."
A little later (V.3.4, 15–7) we learn that discursive reason
understands (*sunesis*) external objects and judges them
by means of standards (*kanosi*) within itself which it has
acquired from intellect.

The phrase "this very power" would seem also to refer
to the lower powers of soul which here, as in Chapter 2, are
accorded some measure of active cognition. But Plotinus
is careful to qualify this ("perhaps"). The ascription of such
powers, even in rudimentary form, to the lower soul is
clearly problematical and whilst Plotinus wants to indicate
that humans have a built-in or innate sense of beauty,
he wishes at the same time to avoid over-complicating
his exposition at this point. And so the vagueness of his
account is to be explained by his unwillingness to over-
burden the main point he is making here (our experience
of *beauty*) with the difficult questions involved in trying
to clarify exactly how a transmission is possible from the

sense-object to discursive reason, questions which are
properly dealt with in the context of sense-perception.

3, 5 For the image of the ruler see also I.8.9, 3; IV.4.23, 39
and V.3.4, 16 above.

3, 9 *the external mass of matter*: Matter, for Plotinus, has no
qualities and is to be identified with total deprivation. It
is the facilitator of three-dimensionality in the sense that
form may, by being reflected on it as on a mirror, create
the manifestation of a three-dimensional world. In this
sense matter enables the existence of "mass" (*ongkos*) which
is the most basic representation of three-dimensionality
before the imposition of more specific forms.

partless though appearing in multiplicity: Even form as present to matter is partless in the sense of physically discrete
parts, but is manifested as having parts. Accordingly, the
physical world of our experience, though not an illusion,
may be regarded as a mere appearance in the sense of a
reflection; and its three-dimensionality is due to matter
reflecting the partless nature of form in three dimensions
and thus diminished in nature.

3, 14 *by now partless*: This phrase is translated by Laurent
by "within" (*eis to eisô*) i.e., the inner (or higher) soul. I
have translated it as referring to "the form in bodies" (line

10), as do Armstrong ("takes it in, now without parts")
and Kalligas.

3, 17–28 Plotinus follows Aristotle (*On the Soul* 418b14–17
and Alexander of Aphrodisias *Commentary on Aristotle
'On the Soul'* 42, 19–43) in believing light to be incorporeal
and supposes this to be Plato's doctrine too (see II.1.7,
23–28, interpreting Plato, *Timaeus* 39b4–5 and 55df.);
see also IV.5.7, 33–41 and IV.5.6, 14 where he suggests
that light is a kind of "activity" (*energeia*); in VI.4.7, 31 it is
described as an "incorporeal power" (*dunamis*); similarly
in I.1.4, 16 soul is said to be present to the body like light,
without being affected. Light, then, is an activity similar
to that of soul or form but not identical with them, just as
fire, on a level lower than that of light, is also not a form
but like a form ("has the rank of form"). Plotinus' theory
of color is expressed here in a way that fits in with his
general argument that beauty is caused at each level by a
cause located at a prior level of reality. So fire possesses
color in a "primary" way, which is then passed on to the
other elements.

3, 17 There are difficulties with the syntax of this sentence.
I have given the noun "shape" a verbal force and, although
taking "masters" to be a noun rather than a verb (the Greek
form permits either), have translated it verbally—literally

"by shaping and by mastering." Kalligas understands "shape" as qualifying "simple."

Shaping: the Greek *morphê* may simply indicate form as denoting a specific color or it might refer to shape. In II.8.1, 12–17 Plotinus entertains the notion that the perception of color brings along with it, in an incidental manner, the awareness of the spatial extent of the color.

by the presence of incorporeal light: For a discussion of the way in which light transmits color see IV.5.7, 37–49, where the presence of light along with matter on which it projects itself produces color. See Emilsson, 1988, 52–55. In II.4.5, 7–12 we have the same contrast between the light provided by form and the darkness of matter. Colors are even described here as being instances of light.

3, 19 *Fire itself is beautiful before all other bodies*: See Plato, *Timaeus* 40a3–4 for the idea that fire is more beautiful and less corporeal than the other three elements, earth, air, and water. But perhaps Plotinus is also equating "fire itself" here with the sun which provides the light that transmits color to physical objects.

3, 26–27 The phrase rendered here as "the fire which does not master" (literally "that which does not master"—*to mê kratoun*) is difficult to translate; it is unclear to what it might refer grammatically in what precedes and it is further unclear what entity Plotinus has in mind. I have taken it, as do Theiler and Igal, as referring to fire. Does he then mean by this inferior manifestations of fire, understanding the highest physical manifestation of fire, which is the first source of light, to be the sun, or does he mean that fire ceases where there is no combustible material, as Igal seems to think (comment *ad loc.*)? The former explanation may be supported by Plotinus' discussion in IV.5.7 of the way in which light is emitted as the external activity of a luminous body such as the sun. At a lower level he mentions the eye as an example of a luminous body that emits light. In the case of some animals this body may itself expand at night emitting much light and contract during the day so that the light is not emitted as strongly. It may then be such a phenomenon which he has in mind with the phrase "that which does not master," i.e., a luminous (fiery) body that has become smaller and less powerful. Armstrong, on the other hand, thinks it refers to dull and ugly colors that sometimes look uglier in bright light and translates: "The inferior thing which becomes faint and dull by the fire's light, is not beautiful any more." Kalligas takes it as referring to perceptible objects which cannot share in the form of color in a complete and perfect way and translates: "While the thing which color does not master, but which fades with the light, is no longer beautiful" (my translation of his modern Greek rendering). Laurent translates: "Ce qui ne s'impose pas [par un éclat particulier] s'efface devant sa lumière et paraît ne plus avoir de beauté." Another solution (Volkmann and Ficino) is to correct *kratoun* to *kratoumenon*, the passive form, "what is not mastered," thus making the phrase refer to whatever is substrate for light and color; McKenna seems to extract the same meaning even by keeping the active form: "And all that has resisted and is but uncertainly held by its light remains outside of beauty." But *kratein* in this treatise at least refers to the power of form to impose itself rather than the resistance (or incapacity) of a substrate to receive form.

3, 28–31 We learn more about musical sound in I.3.1, 20f. where the musical person is seen as easily moved by the beauty in sounds. He is led on from the physical sounds perceived by the senses to the beauty of their intelligible archetypes. It is interesting to note the parallel here between the music lover who is attracted by harmony but avoids its opposite with the lover of beauty in our treatise who recoils from what is ugly.

3, 29 Perhaps an echo of Heraclitus fr. 54, "hidden harmony is better than manifest harmony." See Giannis Stamatellos (2007) for a general account of Plotinus' use of the Presocratics, especially page 162 for hidden harmony and logos.

3, 35 In II.4.5, 18 he describes matter as "an adorned corpse" and uses the same term ("image" *eidōlon*) to designate embodied form.

For "thrilled" see also 2, 9. The expression is a strong one since it seems generally to be used of a violent or disturbing affection, but is evidently used by Plotinus in a positive way as he also employs it to describe the experience of grasping transcendent beauty (4, 14 below).

Chapter 4

He now moves on to the soul's experience of transcendent beauty.

4, 7–9 This stage is one of becoming aware of the manifestations of beauties beyond the physical, but which are still external, that is, in others and not in one's own soul. The following chapter takes up again the distinction between the transcendent beauties we see in others and those that we see in our own souls, an idea that is developed further in Chapter 9 with the striking image of fashioning the statue within ourselves.

4, 10–11 *"splendor"*: Cf. Plato, *Phaedrus* 250b1–3, "splendor of justice and temperance."

"Neither Evening nor . . . so beautiful": The lines are taken from Euripides' *Melanippe* Fragment 486 Nauck (2nd ed.) and include the words "face of justice" according to Nauck. The same lines are found again in VI.6.6, 39. They are cited

by Aristotle (*Nicomachean Ethics* 1129b28–29); but it is evident that Plotinus knows them from a source other than Aristotle, since he gives them in a fuller form, taken probably from Adrastos (see Kalligas *ad loc.*), a Peripatetic philosopher of the 2nd century AD, whose works were among those read in Plotinus' seminars according to Porphyry (*Life of Plotinus* 14).

4, 12 *by that with which the soul sees such things*: The higher part of the soul that contains the forms which enable it to recognize beauty in both physical objects and the incorporeal beauty (of virtues and knowledge) in others.

4, 15 *affections*: Of course the soul does not in fact suffer affections, but such expressions (the words translated here by "experiences" also share the same root word (*pathos*) as "affections") are deliberately chosen by Plotinus to emphasize the power of the experience of beauty at all levels. "Love" is also mentioned here explicitly for the first time, thus introducing this important theme from Plato's *Symposium.* The theme is picked up again at the beginning of the next chapter.

4, 17–22 Armstrong and Laurent take the qualifying phrase *hôs eipein* (literally "so as to say"), which I have translated as "to an extent," with "all" rather than with "experience," meaning that "nearly all" men have this experience, whereas others (MacKenna, Theiler, Kalligas) take it, as I have, to mean "all men have it to some extent."

The statement that all souls have some experience of true beauty may seem surprising since it implies that all men have some insight into intelligible beauty. What he probably means is that physical beauty could not be acknowledged as such at all unless we have some kind of experience, however faint, of its transcendent cause. A similarly positive view lies behind the assertion that we all have the possibility of seeing the intelligible though few go on to attain that goal (see comment on 8, 26–7).

The comparison of the lovers of true beauty with those intensely in love in the physical sense suggests a positive affirmation of physical love (whether this is sexual or more general). (See Introduction, pages 26–31.)

Chapter 5

We are now invited to make a closer examination of incorporeal beauty. It is striking that the immediate object of our enquiry should be the actual experience that we have of beauty, expressed by strong terms of "emotion" ("aroused, stirred, yearn . . .") including that of "love" at different levels. He then changes the tone to a more objective and analytical examination (9). The transition is made from the observation of moral beauty in the actions of others to the inner beauty of their souls and of our own soul. This internal beauty is then identified with being. It will help us to understand its nature if we know what its opposite ugliness is; and this is the subject of the second half of the chapter (from line 24). Ugliness for the soul will turn out to be the addition of worldly accretions which mask the original, pure nature of the soul. The description of this process is very colorful and owes much to Plato and religious notions of the descent and fall of the soul, and leads into the idea of regarding the return of the soul to its original purity as a form of purification, which is the subject of the next chapter. But behind this colorful description of the soul's plight lie two metaphysical considerations:

1. *The understanding of the process of embodiment as the approach of an external element (body?) which attaches itself to soul to produce the compound or embodied soul.*

2. *The important distinction that must be made between embodiment and moral degradation.*

For (1) see VI.4.14, 26 and IV.7 [2] 10 which is expressed in language similar to that found in this treatise, especially the final lines "it [the soul] marveled at what it saw and realized that it needed no beauty applied from outside, since it was itself unsurpassed—provided that it was left to itself" (trans. Fleet).

(2) is based on the idea that the mere embodiment of the soul is not a disorder but part of the necessary fulfilment of the universe. If that is the case, we must exclude any literal interpretation of the present passage as implying that mere attachment to a body entails ugliness of soul and understand all the examples given of "ugliness" as manifestations of purely moral degradation. It is necessary to say this here because Plotinus does often regard the mere descent of soul into body (its primary descent) as, in certain respects, some kind of failure or restricting diminution of its stature; but this is as nothing compared with the further failure of

the individual soul (its secondary descent) to make the most of its physical environment by refusing to surrender to it. Understanding this distinction will help us see more clearly how Plotinus can encourage us to transcend physical beauty and relegate it to an inferior rank but without disparaging it completely. (For the intrinsic value of physical beauty see III.5.1 and Introduction, pages 26–31.) We could say, then, that the relationship of physical beauty to transcendent beauty is similar to that between embodied soul in its primary descent and pure soul.

5, 5 We have already been alerted (2, 10–11) to the idea that the soul contains beauty because it has within it the forms that enable it to recognize physical beauty. But now the emphasis is on the beauty of virtues rather than of the forms of beautiful objects. For internal beauty see Plato, *Phaedrus* 279b9.

5, 6 *aroused*: The Greek (*anabakcheuesthe*) has the strong meaning of "stir up in a Bacchic frenzy." It is found again in VI.7.22, 9 also in the context of "love" at the highest level when the soul receives an "outflow" from the One which "arouses" it to mystical union.

The appeal to a more emotionally and subjectively based experience in these opening lines alerts us to Plotinus' complex understanding of introspection, which is both an intellectual exercise (so from line 9 onward) and the exercising of a more direct experiential encounter with the self. This experiential factor becomes especially pronounced at the level beyond intellect when the soul experiences the One, but can express this verbally or in rational terms only in a way that captures the original experience in image form. See especially VI.7.18–20 and VI.9.3–5, and Smith (1992) VI. 21–30.

5, 10 *"without color"*: A reminiscence of Plato, *Phaedrus* 247c6, where Plato speaks of a transcendent world of being which is without color or shape. Here Plotinus goes beyond Plato, for whom Beauty is one Form amongst others. For Plotinus Beauty has an overriding function of characterizing all Forms as Forms, or archetypes of intelligible order. In this it has the same function as being, which assures the reality of all Forms and their unity as a coherent transcendent entity and is able for this reason to impart to matter the coherence which we observe embodied in the physical world.

5, 19–20 A central idea of this treatise is introduced here, that beauty is identical with being,

5, 22 *like a light*: Plotinus frequently uses the image of light to express the causal effect or external activity of realities on what lies below them, as is implied here with the suggestion that there is some higher cause which casts light over the virtues, i.e. accounts for their beauty. The ultimate source of this obvious image is Plato's analogy of the Sun in the *Republic* 507b–509c. But although usually employed as an analogy, Plotinus also sometimes goes further and identifies this kind of causal activity with light (e.g., VI.7.16, 21–31; V.3.8, 19–25), something we can term "metaphysical" light, akin to, but not identical with, the incorporeal light which illuminates the physical world. See further Beierwaltes 1961 and Smith 2011, 13–19 with the comments of Gurtler 23–26.

5, 32 *a sort of "beauty" brought in from outside*: The person with an "ugly" soul regards, in a perverted way, its "ugliness" to be beauty; in moral terms what is evil would be seen as good. It is "brought in from outside" because beauty is intrinsic to the soul, but may be obscured (see note on 2, 1–10) by evil which originates outside the soul. For the external origin of passions and evil in the soul see IV.7 [2] 10, 7–13.

5, 34 *"jumbled up" with a great deal of evil*: The word and the idea recall Plato, *Phaedo* 66b5.

5, 39–50 These lines might give the impression that Plotinus is referring to the mere embodiment of soul rather than its further failure to prevent itself falling prey to the body. More particularly, the phrase *the things that impinge upon sense-perception* could easily lead to the interpretation that all sense-perception is corrupting, an idea that would negate the value of any experience of physical beauty, which would of necessity have to involve some element of sense-perception. The *mingling and inclination towards body and matter* (48–49) must be interpreted as implying a moral leaning or excessive involvement, which is clear from the reference to *over-familiarity* (55).

form: Must be understood in a weak sense. There is no question of soul taking on a Form of ugliness.

5, 42 *changed*: Strictly speaking, of course, the soul is impassible and cannot change; but allowance must be made for moral "change." Sometimes the word *alloiôsis* as opposed to *kinêsis* is used to express this as here. More generally, moral progression and failure are interpreted by the soul acting or failing to act in accordance with reason and its own nature (see III.6.1–6).

I have here followed Armstrong and Laurent in taking "form that is different from itself" (*eidos heteron*) as the object of "taken into itself" (*eidexamenê*). Others (Theiler, Igal, Kalligas) take it as the object of "changed" (*êllaxato*).

5, 46f. This is perhaps a reminiscence of Plato's description of the earth as opposed to the true heaven and true earth: *Phaedo* 110a5–6, "measureless mud and tracts of mire." But he may also have in mind the sea god Glaucus in the *Republic* (see note on 2, 1–10).

5, 57 *alone*: Does not imply total isolation from all other souls or beings but rather being cut off from all that is inferior or impedes the realization of the true self. See on 6, 11.

5, 58 The *other nature* is matter. See I.8.13, 19 for the same phrase, which expresses the profound otherness of matter from all else.

Chapter 6

6, 1–24 After identifying beauty in the physical world we must next separate our souls from all that is physical, a process which is analogous to "purification" in the religious sense. When soul is dissociated from body in this way (i.e., morally rather than by the physical dissociation which comes with death) it will be seen as being beautiful and the source of beauty. But the next stage, the rediscovery of our intellect, will bring us to an even greater level of beauty, where beauty is identical with being.

6, 1 *ancient tradition*: Plotinus often refers in this way to the philosophical tradition up to the time of Aristotle and, more particularly, to the Pre-Socratics and Plato (e.g., II.9.10, 13; V.1.8, 13). In this case he is probably thinking of Plato, *Phaedo* 69c, which has an Orphic background.

6, 2 There is a long tradition of identifying temperance (*sophrosyne*), courage (*andria*), justice (*dikaiosyne*) and wisdom (*phronesis*) as the four main virtues (although

"justice" is omitted here). These same four are adopted
by Plotinus in I.2 "On Virtue." This tradition goes back
beyond Plato, but is expressed clearly by him in a number of passages. The singling out of "wisdom" (*so also is
wisdom*) may indicate its special position with respect to
the other virtues, an emphasis which goes back to Plato
(Socrates) and was developed by the Stoics, for whom
wisdom is the supreme, and indeed sole, virtue in that it
embraces all the others.

The description of virtues as purifications is taken
from Plato's *Phaedo* 69b–c. See *Ennead* I.2.3–4 where
Plotinus also distinguishes between the purification process itself and the resultant state of purification, a distinction which Porphyry (*Sententiae* 32) formalized into two
distinct phases of moral progress. In V.1.1, 25f. Plotinus
seems to suggest something like two stages, negative and
positive, firstly regarding as contemptible the things which
the soul values in ordinary life, and secondly recognizing
the lofty nature of the soul itself.

6, 6 *just as pigs*: The idea is probably prompted by Plato,
Republic 535d9–5 and Heraclitus DK B13, "Do not revel
in mud. Pigs enjoy mud rather than pure water."

6, 10 For death as the separation of soul from body see
Plato, *Phaedo* 64c5–7.

6, 11 *alone*: This does not refer to living a solitary life, but rather to the life of separation from dependence on external factors. We are reminded of the final words of *Ennead* VI.9, "the flight of the alone to the alone," which alludes to the very highest level of "aloneness," the union with the One which is the ultimate alone. Again the meaning here of personal "aloneness" is of separation from all that is external and less than the inner self. It does not necessarily exclude other "selves," since at this level all "selves" are in a sense one.

Greatness of soul: see Aristotle, *Nicomachean Ethics* 1107b22.

6, 13–24 The line of thought here is not easy to follow. He opens with a statement about the nature of soul in its purest state when it is most fully itself. Since this state is dependent on its being turned toward intellect, he explains what the soul receives from intellect, which is the source to the soul of beauty and the rest of the forms. What soul receives is not alien to its nature because it is in fact truly itself only when it turns toward intellect to receive from it. He can also conclude from this (*"thus it is also correct to say . . ."*) that this state of the soul (as beautiful and good) is what is known as "becoming like god." He now goes further (*"or rather"*) to identify beauty in its fullest sense (beautifulness, *kallonê*) with real being and (with a reference back to Chapter 5: the search for beauty by examining ugliness) concludes (*"so that"*) finally that in God (the One) beautifulness and goodness coincide.

6, 13 *becomes both form and reason principle* . . . : The emphasis on moving from one status to another ("becomes") occurs frequently in Plotinus. In this treatise we may refer to 9.15, 31–32 where Plotinus seems to suggest that we become intellect. In the present chapter he does not seem to go this far, but to hold the individual within the limits of soul. The individual's move from one discrete level of reality to another is more clearly asserted in V.3.4, 10–13 where we are said to "become intellect"; that is, there is a movement within the levels of the self. What moves is less clear; a sort of floating self or focal point which determines the level at which our real lives are conducted. This floating self is not easily accommodated within the structure of traditional Greek metaphysical thought, which is at least one of the reasons why later Neoplatonists were highly critical of Plotinus' concept of an undescended part of the soul.

6, 14–15 *belonging entirely to the divine*: Plotinus is rather loose in the way in which he ascribes divinity to transcendent reality; both the soul and intellect may be said to be divine. Moreover in this passage a distinction is drawn between "belonging to the divine" and the special status of the One which is identified with "god" (lines 20, 23). The reference to god in line 23 neatly concludes the exposition of the ascent of the soul with an implicit reference back to the divinity of soul.

whence: From the divine, that is, intellect.

6, 18 *then*: That is, when the soul is turned toward intellect.

6, 19 We note here the unexpected introduction of "goodness" alongside beauty. It serves in the exposition to link beauty with the Good (the One) which is beyond Intellect and being and reminds us that for Plotinus moral and aesthetic values are intertwined. The same purpose is served by explicitly defining matter (ugliness) as the "primary evil." The next chapter then takes up this theme where it begins with our ascent "to the good." In fact the treatise is gradually extending its range of vision from just beauty to the broader values subsumed under beauty in the transcendent world and their concomitant expressions in our moral stance in this world.

6, 20 *to become like god*: This became the standard aim of the Platonist. It is taken primarily from *Theaetetus* 176b. See David Sedley (1997, 1999).

In this passage "god" who is the source of beauty is to be identified with Intellect rather than with the One, since the following sentence which makes the strong assertion that being, i.e., the Intelligible realm, is not merely the cause of beauty but is identical with it, implies that the "god" to whose likeness we must aspire is Intellect.

6, 21 *Or rather, beautifulness is true being*: He is here making a corrective statement which goes beyond what he has so far said. Up to now the "beauty" referred to is the beauty found in the soul, although it has its source above soul in Intellect. The strong statement now being made is that Intellect or being is identical with beauty. I have translated the Greek *kallonê* by "beautifulness." It is a rare Greek word and otherwise used by Plotinus only in VI.2.18, 1 and VI.7.33, 22, in both cases describing the One. What seems to be happening in our passage is that he begins by affirming the identity of the intelligible world with "beautifulness" but then goes on to suggest in the following lines that it is really in God (the One) that the Good and beautifulness coincide. And the next paragraph (25: "*and we must first posit beautifulness, which is also the Good*") begins with a clear statement identifying the One and beautifulness (see comment below on 26).

6, 24–33 Having traced the ascent of the soul to the beautiful, he now changes direction to follow the impact of beauty on the descending order of levels of reality, beginning with the One, down to the effect of soul on body. This is then picked up at the beginning of the next chapter, where we are encouraged to begin our ascent "once more."

6, 24 *in the same way*: Must refer to the analysis in the preceding section. What is new about the present enquiry is that it seeks to derive beauty as it is manifested at each successive level beginning with its transcendent cause, the "One," i.e. from the top down rather than as before from the physical world upward. We have thus the following schema:

beautifulness/the Good	the One
the beautiful	Intellect
beautiful	soul
beautiful actions, ways of life	sense objects

(There is a problem here: in one sense these manifest themselves physically, in another sense, seen as virtues, they may be divorced from actual instances and therefore be classed as incoporeal states.)

beautiful bodies	sense objects
ugliness	matter

6, 26 *beautifulness . . . intellect*: He now introduces the principle above Intellect, the One, and identifies it with "beautifulness." For the problem of whether to identify beauty with Intellect or with the One, see Chapter 9, 39–43 and the commentary there. The One seems to have been introduced here because of the identification of evil with ugliness (matter) and good with beauty; and since the (Idea of the) Good in Plato is beyond being, the One must now be accorded a role.

6, 29 *as far as they can share in it*: To answer the question why matter does not always reflect all aspects or degrees of Form Plotinus has two strategies: (a) the recipient is not able to receive everything; this is difficult if we are speaking of prime matter, since it would ascribe to it the "positive" property of not being able to receive certain forms; (b) the power of form, each successive level of which is seen as a *logos* or image of its prior, becomes progressively weaker. In this way he can, for example, account (VI.7.9) for the fact that a horse, which does not possess reason, may have as its ultimate cause a Form or intelligible which by definition must have reason (intellect): "For as the powers unfold they always leave something behind on a higher level" (VI.7.9, 38–39, trans. Armstrong).

Chapter 7

Having established more clearly the metaphysical frame-work within which the individual makes his ascent to Intellect and the One, Plotinus now calls on us again, in practical terms, to make the ascent to true beauty and describes what our search for it implies for the way we conduct our earthly lives. He also emphasizes both the basic human urge toward the good and the impact on us of the personal experience of encountering beauty. Both of these are expressed in powerful metaphorical language, for the most part borrowed from Plato's Symposium—*with some additions from the* Timaeus *and* Phaedrus.

7, 1–2 *which every soul desires*: The innate desire for the Good in both the human soul and in the tendency of all reality to seek its perfection in the Good is based ultimately on Plato's insight about the power of "love" in his *Symposium.* For Plotinus it is represented by that inbuilt force which causes all hypostases to cease their outward movement from their producers and to return upon them in contemplation, thus perfecting their own natures. This is seen most crucially in the very first product of the One, Intellect, whose procession (and return) is described in V.2.1, 7ff.: "The One, perfect because it seeks nothing, has nothing, and needs nothing, overflows, as it were, and its superabundance makes something other than itself. This, when it has come into being, turns back upon the One and is filled, and becomes Intellect by looking toward it. Its halt and turning toward the One constitutes being, its gaze upon the One Intellect. Since it halts and turns toward the One that it may see, it becomes simultaneously Intellect and being" (trans. Armstrong, adapted). The human soul strives in the same way to participate in this universal dynamic of procession and return, but without the permanence and timelessness of completely transcendent realities.

7, 2 *Anyone who has seen it*: This appeal to personal experience is important for Plotinus. We learn from VI.9 (see especially VI.9.11) that personal experience of the One, for example, is an important adjunct to discursive arguments which point to it. On this topic see Smith (1992), "Reason and Experience in Plotinus."

7, 5–7 *it is for those who make the* ascent: The reference here to religious ritual recalls the reference to mystery rites in the previous chapter and helps to provide thematic coherence, although a different aspect (that of divesting oneself of garments) is described.

The initial phrase, "divested themselves of the garments they put on in their descent" is syntactically not part of the ritual metaphor, which is introduced with the formula "just as," and must therefore refer to a non-metaphorical process: the idea that the soul, in its descent through the planetary spheres, takes on different faculties like garments. This idea, which was a commonplace, may be found in Porphyry (*Sentences* 29) and would have been familiar to Plotinus' students. Although Plotinus was not generally interested in contemporary religious practice, he does occasionally, as here, make direct and non-critical allusion to it. His employment of such ideas as metaphor, as in the rest of this passage, is more common and unproblematic (and is found in Plato, too, e.g. *Phaedrus* 250b8 and e1). But the direct allusion to non-philosophical ideas has been a source of concern to some interpreters anxious to defend Plotinus' reputation as a "rational" thinker and has led them to an all too ready neglect or even dismissal of them. It is true that Plotinus was less inclined than most of his contemporaries to such ideas; one notes, for example, the clear bafflement of Porphyry [*Life of Plotinus* 10, 37–38] and his fellow students at Plotinus' declaration that "the gods should come to him, not he to them" when asked by Amelius to visit some temples. But it is clear that he could also be sympathetic to the interest of his contemporaries in religious ideas and practices. See, for example, his praise of Porphyry as philosopher and hierophant (*Life* 15, 5), the exploitation of myth (and Platonic myth) in III.5, and his acceptance of the traditional doctrine of the transmigration of souls expressed in a literal rather than metaphorical sense.

7, 9–10 *"unadulterated"*... *"pure"*: Plato, *Symposium* 211e1.

Alone . . . . alone: See note on 6, 11.

7, 10 *from it all depend and to it everything looks*: Expresses a basic tenet of Plotinus' metaphysics, that each level of reality (the One, Intellect, Soul) acts as both the cause and the goal, as efficient and final cause, to what is below it, which is fully constituted by turning back in contemplation of its prior. Life, intellect and being represent an important grouping of concepts which become progressively more systematized by later Platonists as a basic triad employed to structure reality (See Hadot 1957).

7, 14 There is no need to add a negative here with HS_4.

7, 15 *desire*: The same word is used here as for the "desire" of the good expressed at the beginning of the chapter. This expresses the identity of the basic human urge towards beauty and the good.

7, **17** *is struck*: The same word is used by Plato, *Phaedrus* 250a6 for the soul's experience of true beauty. The very physical language used by Plotinus for this experience is inspired largely by Plato.

7, **18–9** *despising what he previously thought was beautiful*: This apparently strong rejection of physical beauty must be seen in context. Elsewhere it is clear that Plotinus values physical beauty in itself (see Introduction), but demotes it, as here, when compared with transcendent beauty. The same ambivalence applies to the material world as a whole when compared with its intelligible archetype.

7, **19–20** *gods or spirits*: See the comment above on 5–7. His reference here is to visible gods such as the stars or spirits that might take on physical appearances, such as the Homeric gods or spirits (*daimones*) that could appear as airy beings. Plotinus seems to be referring to the latter in VI.7.11, 67–9 and further on "*daimones*" see III.5.6.

7, **21–3** *"What then . . . flesh"*: Plato, *Symposium* 211d8–e2.

7, **23** *Not on earth nor in heaven*: Refers respectively to the "other bodies" and the "forms of gods."

7, **26** *gives while remaining in itself*: Another basic metaphysical principle: transcendent realities produce and perfect what is beneath them without being affected or diminished in any way.

7, 30–39 The more extensive significance of the search for beauty and the ultimate purpose of this treatise is now explicitly revealed. For the search for true beauty is now extended beyond transcending physical beauty to include the rejection, too, of all other physical and external goods. This emphasizes the coincidence of true beauty and goodness, and the identification of true beauty with intelligible reality in its entirety. The search for true beauty will lead to moral and spiritual perfection.

7, 31–2 *"prize"* . . . the *"ultimate that is posed to our souls"* . . . *"endeavor"*: Plato, *Phaedrus* 247b5–6.

7, 33 *"blessed sight"*: Plato, *Phaedrus* 250b6.

7, 36 *whose attainment alone*: Plotinus here suggests that external advantages need play no part in the pursuit of happiness, for true happiness may be attained solely by assimilation with god, although the final clause (*"so long as . . ."*) restores some recognition of external goods—they should only be rejected if that is going to assist in realizing true happiness. The treatise I.4 [46], written near the end of his life, contains the most extreme statement of this doctrine where he claims that the good man will be happy even in the bull of Phalaris; for although the empirical self will be suffering (and in the conventional sense "not happy"), the internal contemplation of the man who has attained a higher level of life will be undisturbed. But even in this treatise he still implies a role for external goods and activities, when at the end (I.4.16) he compares the body to a musical instrument that has been given for our use: "And the instrument was not given to him [the good man] in the first place to no purpose; for he has often made use of it up to now." But external goods are, of course, always subordinate to and never supplant the contemplative self-sufficiency of the truly good man.

Chapter 8

In a series of vivid images and allusions we are exhorted to "escape" from the world of lower beauty. The stress is on our own efforts to use the faculty of vision which we all possess.

8, 1–2 *What then is the Way?*: The phraseology of these lines is a play on two texts of Plato: *Philebus* 16b7, where Protarchus begs Socrates to tell him what "way" or "contrivance" (*mêchanê*) he would recommend to extract himself from the difficulties of the argument in which he finds himself, and *Republic* 509a6, where the Idea of the Good is compared with the Sun and is described as an "inconceivable (*amêchanos)* Beauty."

8, 2–3 *which remains, as it were . . .* : Note the sustained cult imagery which helps to unify this with the previous two chapters.

8, 8–16 *like the man who wanted to grasp . . .* : The reference is to the myth of Narcissus, on which see Hadot (1976). For the myth see Ovid *Metamorphoses* 3.339–510, Pausanias

9.31.7–9, Philostratus *Pictures* 1.23. In Plotinus' version, however, Narcissus does not die but slips out of sight into the water. Plotinus is probably thinking of the same myth in the treatise "On Intelligible Beauty," V.8.2, 34–35, "like someone who sees his own image but does not know where it came from and chases after it."

he will consort with shadows both in this life and the next: This conclusion contains a subtle and complex twist. He begins by turning the application of the image away from the purely physical event of drowning into a spiritual one (*"not in body but in soul"*). The watery "depths" are now conceived metaphorically and equated with "Hades." But in the following phrase *he will consort with shadows both in this life and the next* "Hades" is implicitly given two meanings, (1) metaphorical: Hades as this present world in which the non-philosopher will see only images (shadows), and (2) "Hades" in its real sense as the afterlife, which, of course, is peopled by "shadows" (shades). No doubt Plotinus thought that the soul of the philosopher would escape the real Hades, which would remain the location of unenlightened souls after their death.

8, 16 *"Let us flee, then, to our beloved homeland"*: This is a quotation of Homer, *Iliad* 2.140. As often, Plotinus ignores the context of the lines (it is the cry of the Greeks as they seek to abandon the siege of Troy and return home). But the phrase "to our beloved homeland" occurs frequently in the *Odyssey*, which links the quotation more effectively into the context of the *Odyssey* references in the following lines.

8, 18–20 See Homer, *Odyssey* 5,77–268 (Calypso) and 10, 133–574 (Circe). Behind this lies a long tradition of allegorizing Homer as here, for example, in interpreting the journey of Odysseus as the return of the soul to its original home (see Lamberton 1986). Although not mentioned by name, Plotinus probably also has Odysseus in mind when describing the sort of man who succeeds in reaching the intelligible world of the real self, as being "like a man who arrives in his well-governed land after a long journey" (V.9.1, 20–21). Porphyry discourses on the nature of the souls of Odysseus' men who had been transformed by Circe into animals (Fr. 382 Smith) and, in his *Cave of the Nymphs*, a discourse on the meaning of Homer, *Odyssey 13, 102–112,* Odysseus' arrival at the harbor of Phorcys is interpreted as symbolizing the end of the soul's journey home (Chapter 34–35). In the same passage Porphyry expresses his general approval of Numenius' allegorization of the *Odyssey*: "For it is my opinion that Numenius and his school were correct in thinking that for Homer in the *Odyssey*, Odysseus bears a symbol of one who passes through the stages of genesis and, in doing so, returns to those beyond every wave." For Calypso see also Nag Hammadi, NHC II 6,136.27–35.

8, 21 *and there too is our* father: Plotinus frequently calls Intellect or even the One "father," a usage which probably reflects Homer's way of referring to Zeus, and, more immediately, Plato, *Timaeus* 28c3 and 37c7, where the demiurge who creates the world is called "father." For Intellect see V.1.1, 1 and the image of ourselves as "children" separated from their fathers (9–10); II.9.2, 4; 16, 9; and for the One, see V.8.1, 3.

8, 25 *like one shutting his eyes*: The Greek word for "shutting the eyes," *myô*, is from the same root as *mystikos*, although Plotinus here is probably thinking primarily of the physical metaphor of shutting the eyes. See Celsus (in Origen *Against Celsus* 7.39), "Only then will you see god, if you shut your eyes to perceptions and look up with your mind and, turning away the eye of flesh, awaken the eye of the soul." The idea of improved inner vision resulting from diminished external vision also recalls Plato, *Symposium* 219a2–4: "A man's mental vision does not begin to be keen until his physical vision is past its prime."

8, 26–27 *one which everyone possesses*: Plotinus maintains that the highest contemplative level is possible for all men—there are no elite—although few actually manage to achieve it. This optimism is also supported by his doctrine that part of our soul remains undescended, thus providing us with a link which we can use to reach the transcendent. Later Platonists strongly rejected the doctrine of an undescended part of the soul and correspondingly reduced the status of the human soul and its possibility of reaching the intelligible.

Chapter 9

The faculty of vision alluded to at the end of the last chapter is now explained by referring back to the idea of inner sight which is awakened by viewing "external" beauty, which in turn leads us to find true beauty within. When we have fully identified ourselves with the beauty within, we no longer need instruction or philosophical discourse to assimilate ourselves with the ultimate principle. This naturally leads to the question whether Intellect or the One is to be identified with Beauty itself.

9, 2 *when newly stimulated it is unable to see the brightness at all*: This recalls the experience of the freshly escaped prisoner from the cave in Plato's *Republic* 516a, where we have a similar hierarchy of objects to observe before we can view the sun itself. This culminating vision is in fact for Plotinus a complete identification of the self with the light of the sun (see below line 18, where we are said to become the very light itself).

9, 7 *Go back to yourself and see*: With this important injunction Plotinus tells us that intellectual and spiritual awareness are produced not merely by external stimuli but, more importantly, by internal preparation, by making the soul like its objects: in this case making the soul beautiful so that it can more fully perceive beauty. We have already met this idea in 3, 3f., where soul is said to "make a statement by fitting [what it sees] with the form in it. We can compare this with Plotinus' ethical theory, which implies that ethical conduct is both a prerequisite *and* a consequence of contemplative progress. See Smith (1974) 76–77. See also V.8.2, 41–46 for the same idea of seeing oneself beautiful within.

9, 13 *"working on"* . . . *"statue"*: Plato, *Phaedrus* 252d7. In Plato, however, the statue is not the inner self but an image of the "beloved," the object of physical desire. See Armstrong (1961) 112. A similar idea is found in IV.7 [2] 10, 44–47, "For the soul does not, of course, "see wisdom and justice" (Plato, *Phaedrus* 247d6) by making excursions but by contemplation within itself of itself and of what it was formerly, seeing them firmly fixed within itself like statues which have become tarnished with the passage of time and which it has now burnished" (trans. Fleet). Plotinus clearly has in mind the same passage of Plato. See also Porphyry, *Letter to Marcella* 11 (112, 2–5 Des Places), "The wise man . . . must prepare by his wisdom a sanctuary for god in his mind, adorning it with a living statue, intellect, in which god has impressed his image." And Hierocles, a fifth century Platonist from Alexandria (Hierocles, *Commentary on the Golden Verses of Pythagoras* I (31, 21–32, 4 Mullach): "He alone knows how to honor [the gods] who does not contaminate the dignity of those who are honored, and who makes it his foremost concern to present himself as a sanctuary, and works to make his own soul a divine statue and prepares his own intellect as a temple to receive the divine light."

9, 15 *"temperance established on its sacred pedestal"*: Plato, *Phaedrus* 254b7.

"if you have become this": See also lines 21 and 23 below. This notion of becoming identical with the object of striving or of contemplation is central to Plotinus. It is another expression of the idea that true knowledge is found only when the thinking subject is identical with the object of thought (for which see V.5, 1–2). This is valid not only for the hypostasis Intellect but also for the intellect of the individual. This becomes even more complex when viewed dynamically, when he considers the ascent of the individual within the different levels of his own being, from perception to discursive reason (vested in the rational soul), and from discursive reason to intellection. For this transition to complete identity of subject and object at the level of our intellect, see especially the first part of

V.3, which deals with knowing oneself, where in 4, 7–12 he uses the word "becoming" three times to indicate that we "become" completely other than what we were before, in becoming "intellect."

9, 24 *someone to point out the way*: There is a point of transition from discursive reasoning, whether done privately or in the teaching context of the philosophical school, to a direct encounter with the object sought. See VI.9.4, 14–5 where, in speaking of the One, he says that before we have a personal encounter with it our discursive reason "points out the way," "for teaching goes as far as the road and the travelling."

9, 39–43 *So in a rough* sense . . . : The same question arises in the treatise on the *Categories* (VI.2 [43] 18[13]) and that on the Forms and the Good (VI.7 [38] 22), both composed in a later period. Clearly the question, which appears to be cursorily dismissed in I.6, is of some importance to him. In fact it raises difficult issues about the nature of the One as ultimate principle. In some ways Plotinus' strong affirmation of a totally transcendent first principle is the boldest concept of his metaphysics. The relationship of the One to what follows it remained a difficult area of debate for later Neoplatonists. Porphyry seems to have attempted to redefine their relationship, and Iamblichus' One before the One is another way of solving the problem.

We will limit ourselves here to the issue as it arose for
Plotinus in the context of the cause of beauty. While he
raises the question in VI.2, he seems satisfied to identify
Beauty with Being, although he does initially suggest (18,
1–4) that one might locate it somewhat higher, either
with the One itself or rather with something "shining out
from it": "As for the beautiful, if the primary beauty is that
[transcendent First], what could be said about it would be
the same and similar to what was said about the Good;
and if it is that which, one might say, shines out upon the
Idea, [we could say that it is not the same in all] the Forms
and that the shining upon them is posterior." In VI.7,
however, he goes into greater detail. In Chapter 22, while
placing Beauty at the level of Intellect, he suggests that it
receives from the One a kind of illumination which gives
life to that beauty. It should also be noted that, as in I.6,
the immediate context for these comments is the ascent
of the individual soul and its experience of something
above Intellect. But not content with this explanation,
he returns once again to the same issue in Chapter 32,
where he refers to the Good (the One) as the "flower of
beauty" and "another kind of beauty above beauty," and
in 33, 21–3 he says that the "primary beautiful, then, and
the first is without form, and beauty is that, the nature of
the good." Nothing could more clearly express Plotinus'
difficulty in delineating the nature of the One, which he
wants to be not merely the cause of all that is beneath it,

but also in some way to be the totality of everything that exists, an idea most graphically expressed in the opening sentences of V.2 [11] 1: "The One is all things and not a single one of them; it is the principle of all things, not all things, but all things in a transcendent way; for in a sense they do occur in the One." For a more detailed discussion of these passages and the problem of locating Beauty, see Smith (2014).

Select Bibliography

I. Ancient Authors

ALEXANDER OF APHRODISIAS: *Alexander Aphrodisiensis De anima libri mantissa*, ed. Sharples, R. W. 2008. Berlin: De Gruyter.

Alexander of Aphrodisias on the Soul: Part I, trans. Caston, V. 2012. London: Bristol Classical Press.

ARISTOTLE: *Metaphysics*, trans. Ross, W. D. 1928. Oxford: Clarendon Press.

Metaphysica, ed. Ross, W. D. 1957. Oxford: Clarendon Press.

Nicomachean Ethics, trans. Ross, W. D. 1925. Oxford: Clarendon Press.

Ethica Nicomachea, ed. Bywater, L. 1894. Oxford: Clarendon Press.

On the Soul, trans, Smith, J. A. In *The Complete Works of Aristotle in English* (rev. Barnes, J.). 1984. Princeton: Princeton University Press.

De anima, ed. Ross, W. D. 1956. Oxford: Clarendon Press.

Topica, ed. and trans. Forster, E. S. 1989. London: Heinemann (Loeb).

AUGUSTINE: *City of God*, trans. Knowles, D. 1972. Harmondsworth: Penguin.

De civitate dei, ed. Dombart, B. and Kalb, A. 1981. Leipzig: Teubner.

CICERO: *Tusculan Disputations*, ed. and trans. King, J. E. 1966. London: Heinemann (Loeb).

Orator, ed. and trans. Hubbel, H. M. 1939. London: Heinemann (Loeb).

DIO OF PRUSA: *Discourses 12–30*, ed. and trans. Cohoon, J. W. 1939. London: Heinemann (Loeb).

EURIPIDES: *Euripidis Tragoediae superstites et deper-ditarum fragmenta*, ed. Nauck, J. A. 1854. Leipzig: Teubner.

HERACLITUS: In *Die Fragmente der Vorsokratiker I*, ed. Diels, H. and Kranz, W. 1952. Berlin: Weidmann.

Ancilla to the Pre-Socratic Philosophers, trans. of Diels-Kranz fragments, Freeman, K. 1971. Oxford: Basil Blackwell.

HIEROCLES: *In aureum pythagoreorum carmen commentaries,* recensuit et illustravit Frid. Guil. Aug. Mullachius, Berlin. 1853 (reprinted Hildesheim, 1971).

HOMER: *Iliad*, ed. Munro, D. B. and Allen, T. W. 1920. Oxford: Clarendon Press.

Odyssey, ed. Allen, T. W. 1922. Oxford: Clarendon Press.

NAG HAMMADI: *The Nag Hammadi Library in English*, ed. Robinson, J. 2002. Leiden: Brill.

ORIGEN: *Contra Celsum*, ed. and trans. Chadwick, H. 1965. Cambridge: Cambridge University Press.

OVID: *Metamorphoses*, ed. and trans. Miller, F. J. 1916. London: Heinemann (Loeb).

PAUSANIAS: *Description of Greece*, 5 vols. ed. and trans. Jones, W. H. S. 1935. London: Heinemann (Loeb).

PHILOSTRATUS: *Pictures (imagines),* ed. and trans. Fairbanks, A. 1931. London: Heinemann (Loeb).

PLATO: *Opera*, ed. Burnet, J. 1900–1907. Oxford: Oxford University Press.

Collected Dialogues, trans. and ed. Hamilton, E. and Cairns, H. 1963. New York: Pantheon Books.

PORPHYRY: *Lettre à Marcella,* ed. and trans. Des Place, E. 1882. Paris: Les Belles Lettres.

Life of Plotinus in Loeb Plotinus, vol. 1, ed. and trans. Armstrong, A. H. 1969. Cambridge, MA: Harvard University Press.

Sententiae ad intelligibilia ducentes, ed. Lamberz, E. 1975. Leipzig: Teubner.

Pathways to the Intelligibles, English trans. Dillon, J. in *Porphyre Sentences*, tome II, ed. Brisson, L., 2005. Paris: Vrin, pp. 795–835.

PROCLUS: *Elements of Theology*, ed. and trans. Dodds, E. R. 1963. 2nd ed. Oxford: Oxford University Press.

Stoicorum Veterum Fragmenta (SVF): ed. Von Arnim, H. 1905–1924. Leipzig: Teubner.

II. Editions and Translations of the *Enneads*

Armstrong, A. H. 1966–1982. *Plotinus, Enneads*. Greek Text with English Translation and Introductions. 7 vols. Cambridge, MA: Loeb.

Bréhier, Émile. 1924–1938. *Plotin, Ennéades*. Greek Text and French Translation with Introductions and Notes. 7 vols. Paris: Les Belles Lettres.

Cilento, Vincenzo. 1947–1949. *Plotino, Enneadi*. Italian Translation and Commentary. 3 vols. Bari: Laterza.

Creuzer, Georg Friedrich. 1835. *Plotini Enneades*. Greek Text, with Marsilio Ficino's Latin Translation and Commentary. Oxford: E Typographeo Academico.

Brisson, Luc and Jean François Pradeau, eds. 2002–2010. *Plotin Traités*. French Translation and Introductions. 8 vols. Paris: Flammarion.

Harder, Richard, Beutler, Robert, and Theiler, Willy. 1956–1971. Greek Text with German Translation and Commentary. 12 vols. *Plotins Schriften*. Hamburg: Meiner.

Henry, Paul and Schwyzer, Hans-Rudolph. 1951–1973. *Plotini Opera* I-III (editio maior). Paris: Desclée de Brouwer et Cie (HS₁).

Henry, Paul and Schwyzer, Hans-Rudolph. 1964–1982. *Plotini Opera* I-III (editio minor, with revised text). Oxford: Clarendon Press (HS₂).

Igal, Jesus. 1982–1998. *Plotino, Enéadas.* 3 vols. Introduction, translations and notes. Madrid: Gredos.

Kalligas, P. 2006. *Plotinus Ennead I* (in modern Greek). Athens: Akademia Athinon.

Laurent, J. 2002. In *Plotin. Traités 1–6*, eds. Brisson, L. and Pradeau, J.-F. Paris: Flammarion.

MacKenna, Stephen. 1962³. *Plotinus: The Enneads.* English Translation. Revised by B. S. Page. London: Faber & Faber.

———. 1991. *Plotinus. The Enneads.* Selected Treatises Revised with Notes by John Dillon. London: Penguin.

Schwyzer, Hans-Rudolph. 1987. "Corrigenda ad Plotini Textum." *Museum Helveticum* 44, 181–210 (HS₅).

III. Studies on I.6 and Related Works

Anton, John P. 1964. "Plotinus' Refutation of Beauty as Symmetry," In JAAC XXIII: 233–237.

———. 1967. "Plotinus' Conception of the Functions of the Artist." In *The Journal of Aesthetics and Art Criticism* 26: 91–101.

Armstrong, A. H. 1961. "Platonic *Eros* and Christian *Agape*." In *Downside Review* 79: 105–121. (*Plotinian and Christian Studies*. IX. London: Variorum 1979).

Beierwaltes, W. 1961. "Die Metaphysik des Lichtes in der Philosophie des Plotins. In *Zeitschrift für philosophische Forschung* XV: 334–362.

Blumenthal, H. J. 1971. *Plotinus' Psychology. His Doctrines of the Embodied Soul.* The Hague: Nijhoff.

———. 1972. "Plotinus' Psychology: Aristotle in the Service of Platonism." In *International Philosophical Quarterly* XII, 3: 340–364.

Hadot, P. 1957. "Etre, Vie, Pensée chez Plotin et avant Plotin." In *Les Sources de Plotin,* Vendoeuvres: Fondation Hardt, V: 105–141.

———. 1976 "Le mythe de Narcisse et son interpretation par Plotin." Reprinted in *Plotin, Porphyre*. Études néoplatoniciennes. 1999. Paris: les Belles Lettres, 225–266.

Lamberton, R. 1989. *Homer the Theologian*. Berkeley: University of California Press.

Long, A. A. and Sedley, David. 1987. *The Hellenistic Philosophers*, 2 vols. Cambridge: Cambridge University Press.

Miles, Margaret M. 1999. *Plotinus on Body and Beauty*. Oxford: Blackwell.

Sedley, David. 1997. "'Becoming Like God' in the *Timaeus* and Aristotle," in *Interpreting the Timaeus-Critias*, eds. Calvo, T. and Brisson, L. Sankt Anton: Academia Verlag, 327–339.

———. 1999. "The Idea of Godlikeness" in *Oxford Readings in Philosophy. Plato 2*, ed. Fines, G. Oxford: Oxford University Press.

Sheppard, Anne. 1987. *Aesthetics. An Introduction to the Philosophy of Art*. Oxford: Oxford University Press.

Smith, A. 1974. *Porphyry's Place in the Neoplatonic Tradition*. The Hague: Nijhoff.

———. 1992. "Reason and Experience in Plotinus." Reprinted in *Plotinus, Porphyry and Iamblichus: Philosophy and Religion in Neoplatonism*. (2011) VI. London: Variorum.

———. 2011. "Image and Analogy in Plotinus." In *Proceedings of the Boston Area Colloquium in Ancient Philosophy* XXVII: 1–19.

———. 2014. "The Beauty of Divine Intellect in Plotinus." In *The Beauty of God's Presence in the Fathers of the Church* (ed. Rutherford, J. E.). Dublin: Four Courts Press.

Stamatellos, Giannis. 2007. *Plotinus and the Presocratics.* Albany: State University of New York Press.

Wilberding, James. 2006. *Plotinus' Cosmology: A Study of Ennead II.1 (40).* Oxford: Oxford University Press.

IV. General Publications

Alt, K. 1993. *Weltflucht und Weltbejahung. Zur Frage des Leib-Seele Dualismus bei Plutarch, Numenius, Plotin.* Stuttgart: Franz Steiner Verlag.

Armstrong, A. H. 1940. *The Architecture of the Intelligible Universe in the Philosophy of Plotinus.* Cambridge: Cambridge University Press.

Armstrong, A. H., ed. 1967. *The Cambridge History of Later Greek and Early Medieval Philosophy.* Cambridge: Cambridge University Press.

Arnou, R. 1968. *Le Désir de Dieu dans la philosophie de Plotin.* 2nd ed. Rome: Presses de l'Université Grégorienne.

Dillon, J. 1977/1996. *The Middle Platonists: A Study of Platonism, 80 B.C.–A.D. 220*, London: Duckworth, 1977, 1996².

Dodds, Eric R. 1965. *Pagan and Christian in an Age of Anxiety: Some Aspects of Religious Experience from Marcus Aurelius to Constantine.* Cambridge: Cambridge University Press.

Emilsson, E. K. 1988. *Plotinus on Sense-Perception.* Cambridge: Cambridge University Press.

———. 2007. *Plotinus on Intellect.* Oxford: The Clarendon Press.

Gatti, M. L. 1996. *Plotino e la metafisica della contemplazione.* Milan: Vita e Pensiero.

Gerson, L. P. 1994. *Plotinus.* London/New York: Routledge.

———, ed. 1996. *The Cambridge Companion to Plotinus.* Cambridge: Cambridge University Press.

———, ed. 2010. *The Cambridge History of Philosophy in Late Antiquity.* 2 vols. Cambridge: Cambridge University Press.

Gottschalk, H. B. 1980. *Heraclides of Pontus*, Oxford: Oxford University Press.

Guthrie, W. K. C. 1967–1978. *A History of Greek Philosophy*, 5 vols. Cambridge: Cambridge University Press.

Hadot, Pierre. 1993. *Plotinus on the Simplicity of Vision.* Translated by M. Chase. Chicago: Chicago University Press.

Inge, W. R. 1948. *The Philosophy of Plotinus.* 3rd ed. London: Longmans, Green.

Les Sources de Plotin. 1960. Entretiens Fondation Hardt V. Vandoeuvres-Genève.

Lloyd, Anthony C. 1990. *The Anatomy of Neoplatonism.* Oxford: Clarendon Press.

Meijer, P. A. 1992. *Plotinus on the Good or the One (Enneads VI, 9): An Analytical Commentary.* Amsterdam: J. C. Gieben.

O'Daly, G. 1973. *Plotinus' Philosophy of the Self.* Shannon: Irish University Press.

O'Meara, Dominic J. 1993. *Plotinus: an Introduction to the Enneads.* Oxford: Oxford University Press.

Pépin, J. 1958. *Mythe et allégorie: les origins grecques et les contestations judéo-chrétiennes.* Paris: Aubier.

Remes, Pauliina. 2007. *Plotinus on Self: The Philosophy of the 'We.'* Cambridge: Cambridge University Press.

Remes, Pauliina. 2008. *Neoplatonism.* Berkeley: University of California Press.

Rist, John M. 1967. *Plotinus: The Road to Reality.* Cambridge: Cambridge University Press.

Schniewind, Alexandrine. 2003. *L'Éthique du Sage chez Plotin.* Paris: J. Vrin.

Smith, A. 1974. *Porphyry's Place in the Neoplatonic Tradition: A Study in Post-Plotinian Neoplatonism,* The Hague: Nijhoff.

Smith, A. 1981. "Potentiality and the Problem of Plurality in the Intelligible." In *Neoplatonism and Early Christian Thought,* eds. H. J. Blumenthal and R. A. Markus. London: Variorum, 99–107.

Smith, A. 2004. *Philosophy in Late Antiquity.* London: Routledge.

Theiler, W. 1960. "Plotin zwischen Platon und Stoa." In *Les Sources de Plotin*, Entretiens Fondation Hardt V, Vandoeuvres-Genève: Fondation Hardt, 63–103.

Wallis, R. T. 1995. *Neoplatonism.* 2nd ed. London: Duckworth.

West, M. L. 1966. *Hesiod* Theogony, *Edited with Prolegomena and Commentary.* Oxford: Clarendon Press.

Index of Ancient Authors

137

Index of Names and Subjects

PRE-SOCRATICS

By Being, It Is: The Thesis of Parmenides by Néstor-Luis Cordero

The Fragments of Parmenides: A Critical Text with Introduction and Translation, the Ancient Testimonia and a Commentary by A. H. Coxon. Revised and Expanded Edition edited with new Translations by Richard McKirahan and a new Preface by Malcolm Schofield

The Legacy of Parmenides: Eleatic Monism and Later Presocratic Thought by Patricia Curd

Parmenides and the History of Dialectic: Three Essays by Scott Austin

Parmenides, Venerable and Awesome: Proceedings of the International Symposium edited by Néstor-Luis Cordero

Presocratics and Plato: A Festschrift in Honor of Charles Kahn edited by Richard Patterson, Vassilis Karasmanis, and Arnold Hermann

The Route of Parmenides: Revised and Expanded Edition, With a New Introduction, Three Supplemental Essays, and an Essay by Gregory Vlastos by Alexander P. D. Mourelatos

To Think Like God: Pythagoras and Parmenides. The Origins of Philosophy. Scholarly and fully annotated edition by Arnold Hermann

The Illustrated To Think Like God: Pythagoras and Parmenides. The Origins of Philosophy by Arnold Hermann with over 200 full color illustrations

PLATO

A Stranger's Knowledge: Statesmanship, Philosophy, and Law in Plato's Statesman by Xavier Márquez

God and Forms in Plato by Richard D. Mohr

Image and Paradigm in Plato's Sophist by David Ambuel

Interpreting Plato's Dialogues by J. Angelo Corlett

One Book, the Whole Universe: Plato's Timaeus Today edited by Richard D. Mohr and Barbara M. Sattler

Platonic Patterns: A Collection of Studies by Holger Thesleff

Plato's Late Ontology: A Riddle Resolved by Kenneth M. Sayre

Plato's Parmenides: Text, Translation & Introductory Essay by Arnold Hermann. Translation in collaboration with Sylvana Chrysakopoulou with a Foreword by Douglas Hedley

Plato's Universe by Gregory Vlastos

The Philosopher in Plato's Statesman by Mitchell Miller

ARISTOTLE

Aristotle's Empiricism: Experience and Mechanics in the Fourth Century B.C. by Jean De Groot

One and Many in Aristotle's Metaphysics—Volume I: Books Alpha-Delta by Edward C. Halper

One and Many in Aristotle's Metaphysics—Volume 2: The Central Books by Edward C. Halper

Reading Aristotle: Physics VII.3 "What is Alteration?" Proceedings of the International ESAP-HYELE Conference edited by Stefano Maso, Carlo Natali, and Gerhard Seel

HELLENISTIC PHILOSOPHY

A Life Worthy of the Gods: The Materialist Psychology of Epicurus by David Konstan

THE ENNEADS OF PLOTINUS

Translations with Introductions & Philosophical Commentaries

Series edited by John M. Dillon and Andrew Smith

Ennead II.5: On What Is Potentially and What Actually by Cinzia Arruzza

Ennead IV.3–IV.4.29: Problems concerning the Soul by John M. Dillon and H. J. Blumenthal

Ennead IV.4.30–45 & IV.5: Problems concerning the Soul by Gary M. Gurtler

Ennead IV.8: On the Descent of the Soul into Bodies by Barrie Fleet

Ennead V.1: On the Three Primary Levels of Reality by Eric D. Perl

Ennead V.5: That the Intelligibles are not External to the Intellect, and on the Good by Lloyd P. Gerson

Ennead VI.4 & VI.5: On the Presence of Being, One and the Same, Everywhere as a Whole by Eyjólfur Emilsson and Steven Strange

ETHICS

Sentience and Sensibility: A Conversation about Moral Philosophy by
Matthew R. Silliman

PHILOSOPHICAL FICTION

Pythagorean Crimes by Tefcros Michaelides

*The Aristotle Quest: A Dana McCarter Trilogy. Book 1: Black
Market Truth* by Sharon M. Kaye

AUDIOBOOKS

The Iliad (unabridged) by Stanley Lombardo

The Odyssey (unabridged) by Stanley Lombardo

The Essential Homer by Stanley Lombardo

The Essential Iliad by Stanley Lombardo

FORTHCOMING

*Plato in the Empire: Albinus, Maximus, Apuleius. Text, Translation,
and Commentary* by Ryan C. Fowler

Ennead I.1: What is the Living Being, and What is Man?
by Gerard O'Daly

Ennead I.2: On Virtues by Suzanne Stern-Gillet

Ennead I.3: On Dialectic by Pauliina Remes

Ennead I.4: On Well-Being by Kieran McGroarty

Ennead II.4: On Matter by Anthony A. Long

Ennead II.9: Against the Gnostics by Sebastian Ramon Philipp Gertz

Ennead III.5: On Love by Sara Magrin

Ennead III.7: On Eternity and Time by László Bene

Ennead III.8: On Nature and Contemplation by George Karamanolis

Ennead IV.7: On the Immortality of the Soul by Barrie Fleet

Ennead V.3: On the Knowing Hypostases by Marie-Élise Zovko

Ennead V.8: On Intelligible Beauty by Andrew Smith

Ennead V.9: On Intellect, Ideas, and Being by Matthias Vorwerk

Ennead VI.8: On Free Will and the Will of the One
by Kevin Corrigan and John D. Turner